HOW TO MAKE YOUR GARDEN GROW

HOW TO MAKE YOUR GARDEN GROW

A beginner's guide to the planting and care
of popular garden plants

Toby and Lisa Buckland
Photographs by Howard Rice

MITCHELL BEAZLEY

For Henry, Eddie and Emma-Rose

The photographer would like to offer special thanks to the following garden owners:

Kathy Brown, The Manor House, Stevington, Bedford: 33 br; Cambridge University Botanic Garden: 26/27,148/149; Clare College, Cambridge: 94/95; Sally and Don Edwards, Horningsea, Cambridge: 72/73; Bob and Sue Foulser, Cerne Abbas, Dorset: 126/127; New Hall College, Cambridge: 52/53; The Royal Horticultural Society, Wisley Garden: 111.

How To Make Your Garden Grow

by Toby and Lisa Buckland

First published in Great Britain in 2004 by Cassell Illustrated

This edition published in 2009 by Mitchell Beazley,
an imprint of Octopus Publishing Group Ltd,
2–4 Heron Quays, London E14 4JP
An Hachette UK Company
www.hachettelivre.co.uk

ISBN: 978 1 84533 505 2

A CIP record for this book is available from the British Library

Set in Avenir

Colour reproduction by AltaImage
Printed and bound in China by Toppan Printing Company Ltd

Editorial and Design:
Pippa Rubinstein & Judith Robertson
R & R Publishing

Contents

INTRODUCTION 7
CLIMATE & HARDINESS ZONES 7

1 GARDENING TECHNIQUES 8
Tool Starter Kit 10
Shopping 12
Soil Improvement
and Feeding 14
Planting Out 16
Watering 18
Weeding and Tidying 20
Staking and Protecting
Your Plants 22
Sowing Plants from Seed 24

2 YEAR-ROUND STRUCTURE 26
Bamboo 28
Sweet Bay 30
Box 32
Cordyline and Phormium 34
Willow and Dogwood 36
Euphorbia 38
Japanese Maple 40
Lavender 42
Ceanothus 44
Chusan Palm 46
Tree Fern 48
Plant a Lavender Hedge 50

3 FLOWERS WITH IMPACT 52
Drumstick Allium 54
African Lily 56
Foxtail Lily 58
Bearded Iris 60
Foxglove 62
Lily 64
Tulip 66
Canna Lily 68
Get the Tropical Look 70

**4 SUMMER CLIMBERS &
& BACKDROPS 72**
Banana 74
Clematis 76
Annual Climbers 78
Fig 80
Roses 82
Sweet Pea 84
Delphinium 86
Hollyhock 88
Classic Rose Training 90

5 FLOWERS TO FILL SPACES 92
Hellebore 94
Aquilegia 96
Herbaceous Peony 98
Poppy 100
Cosmos 102
Day Lily 104
Crocosmia 106
Dahlia 108
Red Hot Poker 110
Rudbeckia 112
Salvia 114
Penstemon 116
Michaelmas Daisy 118
Garden Chrysanthemum 120
Grow Flowers for Cutting 122

6 EDGERS & SOFTENERS 124
Artemisia 126
Hardy Geranium 128
Ornamental Grasses 130
Heuchera 132
Hosta 134
Marguerite 136
Nepeta 138
Pelargonium 140
Sedum 142
Create an Annual Meadow 144

7 FLOWER CARPETS 146
Anemone 148
Daffodil 150
Snowdrop 152
Viola 154
Wallflower 156
Glossary 158
Index 160

Introduction

This is a book for people who love plants – seeking them out, planting them and watching them grow and do their thing. Whether you're a beginner or a seasoned gardener, the beauty of gardening is that there is always more to learn. In this book you'll find not just the usual information about how tall and wide a plant will get and if and when it flowers, but how to use it in your borders, pots and boundaries. After all, it's just as important to know what a plant can do – whether it will spread to suppress weeds or froth into a screen to block out the neighbours. You'll also find lots of practical tricks of the trade to improve your plants and make caring for them a doddle.

I have taken the headache out of selecting and growing plants, showing in step-by-step format what they need, how to do it and when. I have included only the plants that perform well in my own garden. These are my favourites, hand-picked

This book will teach you how to give your garden plants the right care at the right time.

performers that look good together throughout the year. After all, you don't need to include every plant that exists to have a colourful garden, just a small, well-grown selection of the best.

Because so much of the fun of gardening is about being creative, I have included lots of ideas on using and designing with plants, and there's a project at the end of each chapter that I hope you'll find inspiring!

So, if you've ever stood with a plant pot in your hand at the garden centre, trying to make sense of the label, then this book is for you. It's also for you if you've ever looked out at your garden and wondered how to make it more colourful, more interesting or just wished for ideas on what to plant where.

Don't let past mistakes or the fear of making new ones put you off. Getting your garden to grow is without doubt one of the most natural and enjoyable ways of spending your time. Learn to do it well and your plants will flourish.

CLIMATE & HARDINESS ZONES

The average winter temperature is the factor that determines whether a plant endures in your garden or not and this comes down to your geographical location. If your garden is near the coast, winters will be mild, whereas gardens locked in by thousands of miles of land or in mountainous regions get very cold.

To give an indication of just how cold the average temperature gets, the United States Department of Agriculture has developed a map dividing North America into plant hardiness zones (a similar map has been adopted for Europe). These range from a chilly zone 1 with an average winter temperature below –4°C (–50°F) to the sweltering zone 10 with winter temperatures of 4–6°C (39–43°F). So a plant with a zone 8 tag will, in theory, grow in all the zones from 8 upwards and should, with a little winter protection, survive in zone 7.

However, more important still are local factors such as rainfall figures, soil type and proximity to rivers, forests and cities. All these things create microclimates that broaden or shrink the range of plants you can grow. To find out about your local microclimate you need to tap into local knowledge and ask for information at your nearest nursery or open garden.

As a broad guide, the UK, lowland France and Germany, and the East and West Coast USA fall into zones 8 and 9 and all plants in this book are worth trying there. The Rockies, Northern USA, Canada and Eastern Europe are in zones 3 to 5

Tools

Shopping

Planting out

CHAPTER 1

Gardening Techniques

Gardeners tend to fall into two categories: those who plant first, then read up about it later, and those who read everything there is about their plants and then do it by the rules. There's no right or wrong here, both will admit to their fair share of successes and failures. Gardening isn't an exact science, but that's what makes it fun, challenging and rewarding.

This chapter provides information on some basics, like what to look for when buying plants and tools, and how to weed, water and feed to help if you're just starting out, plus tricks of the trade if you want to learn a bit more.

You will also find everything you need to know about growing our plant selection, such as how to sow annuals and biennials and and how to keep those tender types alive through winter. Bear in mind that gardening is as much about confidence as knowledge, so don't be afraid to have a go and learn by experimenting.

Propagating

Weeding

Tool Starter Kit

When you're starting out, a spade is probably the first tool you'll buy, and it'll get you a long way – from cutting out borders from the lawn and digging them over, to improving the soil and planting. If you buy a fork and watering can at the same time, the rest of the tools can wait. It's always worth spending as much as you can to buy quality tools which last longer and are more comfortable than short-lived 'bargains'. Spades and forks, especially, come in dozens of designs – some with long handles, some light, some purposely heavy to suit all shapes and sizes of gardener. So find one that suits you.

YOU WILL NEED

- **Hand fork** – For hand-weeding around plants, dividing small plants – buy one with flat tines rather than the claw type.

- **Trowel** – For planting bulbs, bedding in small perennials, for digging out deep weeds.

- **Secateurs** – For deadheading, pruning and taking cuttings.

- **Spring-tine rake** – For raking leaves and tidying up, combing out dead growth from ornamental grasses.

- **Dutch hoe** – For fast weeding borders on sunny days in summer.

- **Large and small watering can** – Two sizes are always good because small, long-necked cans offer greater control and direction for small pots, greenhouse cuttings and seedlings; use large cans for speedy watering of bigger pots and borders.

- **Spade** – For digging and improving soil, planting and dividing plants (don't confuse with a shovel, which is wider and angled for scooping not digging!).

- **Gloves** – For pulling out nettles and thistles, working with roses, and essential for pregnant women to protect against infection from toxicara worms which are spread in cat faeces.

Secateurs and a hand
fork and trowel are a
good place to start
when buying tools

● Wheelbarrow – Probably one of the
most useful tools there is if you have a
tennis court-size garden and above.
For barrowing compost and prunings,
for collecting weeds, helping with
watering, moving heavy pots for
overwintering and much more. Always
plump for a builder's barrow from a
builder's hardware store, as they're
robust, comfortable to push and the
best value.

Shopping

For many gardeners shopping is one of the great pleasures of gardening, while for others it's a necessary evil! These days there are more ways to shop for plants than ever – by post and internet, with a huge range of choice in the container-grown market. Some people say you should never buy a plant unless you know where it's going, but where's the fun in that? It's only natural to give in to impulse occasionally, just don't let them languish in pots outside your back door. Better to get them into the ground – even in the wrong place – then you can always move them later.

MAIL ORDER

For a wider range of more unusual plants at a reasonable price, it's worth seeking out specialist nurseries who'll deliver plants to your door, often as bare-root, bulbs or boxed-up young plants. The internet, garden shows and the back of gardening magazines are the place to find them. With any plant that comes wrapped up, get them out of the packaging as soon as possible – if you can't plant bulbs immediately, keep them somewhere cool, such as an outdoor shed (as long as its mouse-free!).

A calendar for ordering:
- Early to late spring
for seeds and bedding plugs.

- Late spring/early summer
for perennials and climbers.

- Late summer/autumn
for spring bulbs.

- Autumn through to spring
for summer bulbs, woody plants, hedging and bare-root perennials.

CONTAINER-GROWN

Go into any garden centre and there'll be lots of container-grown plants in flower. Buying like this helps with colour scheming, and if you go every few weeks, will give you a garden with flowers in every month of the year. But this isn't the only way to buy …

BUY LARGE PLANTS FOR INSTANT IMPACT

Not that long ago, if you wanted a large plant you had to grow it, but these days almost everything is available as a large container-grown plant. Design-wise they have the advantage of instant impact and you only need one to change the whole feel of a garden. The downside is they're expensive and they require the best planting and aftercare. You'll have to dig a very large hole, and may have to replace the subsoil with extra soil and compost.

Large shrubs and trees, such as the Chusan palm, topiary box and bay, should always be staked to support them for the first year. During this time they'll need to be watered well with a hosepipe on a slow trickle whenever the weather turns dry.

When planting large containers, rope in friends or neighbours to help and to save your back. Manoeuvre the rootball into the hole using a plank as a slipway.

PLUG PLANTS

Plug plants – rooted cuttings or seedlings – have taken over from seeds in the plant stakes as a way to grow bedding, such as pelargoniums, cosmos and violas. More expensive than seed, but still economical compared to larger pot-grown plants, it makes sense to buy these plants small as they grow fast and will flower in their first year anyway.

True to their name, their roots grow in plugs of compost held in place with netting. When you get them home, remove all external packaging (not netting though) and plant immediately into 8cm (3in) pots. If you're buying before frosts have finished, make sure you have somewhere frost-free and bright to keep them until you plant them into bigger pots, baskets or the border.

Soil Improvement and Feeding

Think about soil improvement and feeding as being a circular process. It starts in spring with getting the soil ready by digging it over to banish weeds, and then enriching it with compost. Once the plants are in the ground, fast-growing types and abundant flowerers need regular feeding to fuel their rapid growth and to top up the reserves that are being taken from the soil. Then it's back to feeding the ground in autumn with compost. But now you simply spade it on to the surface in a 5cm (2in) layer and let the worms work it into the soil.

DIGGING IN COMPOST

All uncultivated soils need improving before you plant, whether clay, chalky or sandy.

If you're not sure which soil type you have, don't worry. Whether it dries out too quickly or gets waterlogged in winter, it can only be improved by digging in lots of nourishing compost.

All compost is rotted-down plant material. You can make your own by stacking up your grass clippings, leaves and prunings and letting them rot in a heap. Alternatively, you can buy bags of soil improver made from a mix of composted bark, rotted-down leaves and chippings. If you can get hold of it, well-rotted manure is best of all as it improves the soil and has higher levels of important nutrients.

Blend the compost into the soil with a spade and then a fork, incorporating up to half a barrow per square metre (or yard), and digging it in to the depth of the fork's prongs.

FEEDING PLANTS

Gardeners want their plants to be bigger, bolder and flower for longer than they would in the wild and that's where fertilizer comes in. There are different types depending on where plants are grown. Use balanced fertilizers to pep up new borders and to feed the soil before planting bedding plants. Liquid fertilizers are good in summer as an instant boost for plants that aren't growing or flowering well. For a long-term feed in containers and borders, sprinkle slow-release pellets between plants in spring and again in high summer. For flowerpots, use a tomato feed, where the balance of nutrients is specifically designed to encourage flowering. In spring and summer, liquid seaweed sprayed on to the leaves of roses will help keep them healthy.

TRICKS OF THE TRADE

- If your soil is wet and sludgy under foot, even in summer, add half a bucket of grit to the dug-up soil before firming it back around plants. Mounding soil up so that the crowns of the plants are 5cm (2in) higher than the surrounding ground will help too.

- Shredding plant stems and woody prunings before putting on the compost heap guarantees that they will rot down quickly.

- Clay soils are best dug in early autumn when they have enough moisture to make them soft but not too sticky.

- When you dig, start at one end of your border and work backwards. When you've finished, knock any lumps apart with a fork, rake it level and tread with the soles of your boots close together to firm it up and prevent it soaking up rain like a sponge.

WHAT'S IN FERTILIZER?

Plants need a range of nutrients to grow well and fertilizers contain various mixes to suit different plants. The main ingredients (needed by plants regularly) are nitrogen (N), which promotes leafy growth, phosphate (P), which encourages roots and potassium (K) for flowering and fruit.

On the box of fertilizer you'll see these represented as numbers, for example N10, P10, K10. If they are all the same, the fertilizer is described as balanced. If one nutrient has a higher number than the rest, that aspect of the plant's growth will be encouraged. In addition to the main nutrients, you will find the more expensive fertilizers contain extra trace elements, which are required by plants in minute quantities.

MULCHING

Like digging but without turning the soil, mulching is the way to improve soil where plants are already growing. Use compost, well-rotted manure or composted bark and cover the ground to a depth of 5cm (2in) in either spring or autumn. The only rule is to make sure the soil is moist before applying it and then the mulch will seal in the water. Over time, worms will digest the mulch and move it down among the roots. So for maximum benefit, top up levels every year.

TYPES OF FERTILIZER

- **Pelleted chicken manure** – High in nitrogen so gives a boost to leafy growth in spring and summer.

- **Growmore** – A balanced fertilizer good when cultivating new ground.

- **Fish, blood and bone** – The organic version of Growmore.

- **Controlled release** – Pellets that respond to ambient temperatures, releasing more nutrients as the weather warms and plants grow faster. Expensive but ideal for pots.

- **Comfrey feed** – Home-made organic version of fertilizer made by steeping comfrey leaves in water.

- **Tomato fertilizer** – Blended to encourage flowers and the production of fruit.

- **Seaweed** – Containing trace elements this is the feed to use for general plant health. Also contains iodine to deter pests and fungal diseases.

Planting Out

When it comes to planting, don't rush it. No matter how eager you are to get new flowers in your garden, never plant when the ground is frozen or if it's really wet. It's always worth taking time over soil preparation, watering and a little tending until a new plant is established.

1 SOAK POTS

Before planting, soak pots in a bucket of water or barrow for 15 minutes. It's the best way to make sure container-grown plants are sufficiently moist before going in the ground.

2 SET OUT PLANTS

If you've bought a lot of plants, don't plant one at a time. Set all the pots out on the soil surface first, shuffling them round if necessary and taking time over spacing while considering colour combinations. Avoid planting in lines – triangles look more natural, and don't feel that all large plants need to be at the back. Those like delphiniums, which have tall flowerheads but low clumps of leaves, are fine mid border surrounded by other flowers. Keep the labels for reference.

3 DIG A HOLE

With a spade, dig a hole about twice the size of the pot. If you haven't already improved the soil, fork half a bucketful of garden compost or soil improver into the base, and sprinkle a few handfuls over the dug-up soil.

4 KNOCK THE PLANT OUT OF THE POT

Next, knock the plant out of its pot. The best way is to turn it upside down in one hand and firmly tap the rim with the heel of your other hand.

5 TEASE OUT ROOTS

If roots are growing in circles around the base of the pot, loosen them to encourage them to grow out into the soil. Concentrate on teasing out the ones at the base.

6 PLANT AT THE RIGHT HEIGHT

Set the plant down into the hole. The level of the compost should be the same as that of the surrounding soil (except for crocosmia, roses and clematis). If you find it hard to see the level by eye, check by spanning the hole with a bamboo cane and add or remove soil until the level's right.

7 BACKFILL THE SOIL AND FIRM IN

Push soil back in around the plant with your fingers, making sure there are no air gaps between roots and soil. Firm down the soil with the ball of your foot, gently rocking from one foot to the other right round the plant. You can tell if it's in firmly enough, because it shouldn't budge if tugged.

8 WATER

Finally, pour on half a can of water to wash soil down around the roots. Keep watering whenever it gets dry and baking hot. If you're unsure whether there's moisture in the ground, dig down with a trowel to check.

Watering

If only it rained every night and was sunny every day, you'd never need to water, but every garden needs to be watered from time to time, and newly bought plants and summer pots may need water daily. Some soils are thirstier than others, so follow the advice in 'Soil Improvement' (*see* pages 14–15) before you start as this can increase water retention. Accepted wisdom says it's best to water in the evening when there is less evaporation, but don't delay if a plant is wilting before your eyes. Remember, it's not just sun that makes plants wilt, very windy weather sucks moisture out just as fast.

HOW OFTEN SHOULD I WATER?

Do a test to see how often to water by digging down between plants with a trowel. If the top few inches are dry, you need to roll out the hosepipe. Learn to recognize stress signs (even before plants wilt) without having to dig, such as pale, dusty-looking soil and a lack of lustre in leaves.

HOW MUCH WATER?

Combine the dig-down test with a sprinkler test by leaving it on to see how long water takes to soak down into soil and use that as your guide.

Remember, concentrate water around the base of your plants so that it goes right down to the roots.

Attach waterbutts to downpipes and use the harvested rainwater for border plants and containers, but not seedlings.

NEW PLANTS

Rootballs that get planted dry tend to stay dry, so give pots a good soak in a bucket of water before planting. When the compost stops bubbling, they are ready to plant.

YOUNG PLANTS

Small plants and seedlings need more gentle watering to avoid washing compost from pots and dislodging roots, so fix a rose to the spout of the watering can to create a soft shower.

EASY POTS

When planting up summer pots, adding a few teaspoons of water-retaining crystals (widely available from garden centres) to the compost cuts down on how often you need to water.

DIY SPRINKLER

Free up time spent watering by propping a spray gun in the handle of a garden spade and leaving it to give thirsty beds a good soak for a few hours.

HOME ALONE

Every gardener has newly bought plants waiting outside the back door to go in the garden. Loading them into a wheelbarrow with a couple of inches of water in the base stops them drying out, particularly if you are going away on holiday.

TIPS

PRESERVING PLANTS IN POTS

As a general rule, hanging baskets, window boxes and anything smaller than a 18cm (12in) pot needs watering once or twice a day in hot spells in summer, whereas half-barrels and larger can go up to a week without watering in summer.

If small pots dry out totally, place them in a barrow of water to soak for half a day. If wet weather conspires to overwater plants, dry out the compost quickly by taking plants out of the pot for a few hours.

Weeding and Tidying

For an interesting and colourful garden, packing it with your favourite plants and flowers is only half the story … you've got to keep it looking good and that means pruning, tidying and a little weeding. Don't think that this means constant maintenance (although the little and often approach does work). Try to blitz borders, pulling out unwanted weeds and trimming back unwanted growth at least once in every season, and spend the rest of the time pottering, deadheading and sitting back to enjoy the view.

WEEDING

If you're starting a new border, make sure it's weed-free before you plant as it'll save time later on. That's easier said then done, particularly with invasive perennial weeds, such as bindweed and ground elder, that spread quickly and have hard-to-rid roots. Unless you are prepared to repeatedly use a weedkiller – and this won't work if weeds are spreading under the fence from a neighbour's garden – you need design solutions. One is to grass over the weedy area and keep mowing it. After a year of this even the most dogged weed will give up the ghost. Another organic method is to create a low raised bed on top of the weedy bed, lined with permeable weed-suppressing membrane to allow moisture through, but not the weeds. Again, excluding light will see the offenders off and allow you to grow plants in the meantime.

Few of us have the time for a manicured garden or the stomach for using chemicals to make it

weed free, and having a few weeds – some people call them wildflowers – isn't the end of the world. Just make sure you get the balance in favour of your plants right – never allow weeds to seed or dominate, getting first dibs of food, light and water.

The organic approach is to dig out weeds by hand or cover the area with black plastic weed

matting that you can buy off the roll from the garden centre. It's not fast, though, as the earth needs to be covered for at least a year.

Once the border's planted, annual weeds will appear, but are easy to pull or hoe off when the soil is dry. If you choose a sunny, breezy day cut stems will wither before they can re-root.

TIDYING AND BLITZES

SPRING – Before perennials come fully into growth, spend a day going through borders pulling weeds from the crowns of plants, and among seedlings of self-sown plants that you want to keep, such as poppies or hellebores. Cut back any overwintered stems from last year down to the base to make way for the new. A good tip is to have a look over the border before you start so you avoid crushing spring and summer bulbs underfoot.

SUMMER – In the chaos of summer growth, don't forget fledgling plants, especially if they neighbour fast-growing types. Keep the area around them trimmed so they get plenty of light and rain. By early summer, flowers like aquilegias and common foxgloves have finished and unless you want them to seed, be ruthless about cutting them down or pulling them out altogether. You can safely pull out the foliage of spring bulbs too as they will have had enough time to replenish the bulbs for the winter by now.

AUTUMN – This is the biggest tidying session of the year, but it's as much about what you leave as what you prune. Weather-worn perennial stems should be cut down right to ground level, to show off those that are still standing, such as deciduous grasses and rudbeckias. Other candidates to leave unpruned are tender plants, such as penstemon (in some areas) to act as a layer of insulation and protect the crown from the worst of the cold. Also cut down diseased stems, notably rusty-leaved hollyhocks, and save for the bonfire. Then mulch around the plant to prevent spores being splashed back into the crown by rain.

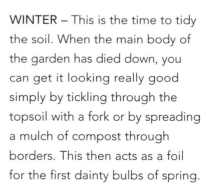

WINTER – This is the time to tidy the soil. When the main body of the garden has died down, you can get it looking really good simply by tickling through the topsoil with a fork or by spreading a mulch of compost through borders. This then acts as a foil for the first dainty bulbs of spring.

Staking and Protecting Your Plants

Your plants need you! When small, they're most vulnerable and even when they've grown up, if conditions outside are hard and extreme, they can be hurt. If you know the risks, though, you're halfway to keeping them healthy and alive.

WINDY WEATHER

Herbaceous plants are prone to being blown over in strong wind, especially those with very tall stems and large heavy flowers. The best time to stake is before the plants are above 30cm (1ft) tall in mid spring as this way they grow through and hide the supports as the season progresses.

Leave it until plants are larger, and it's impossible to disguise the stakes. That's why it's a good idea to use natural twigs and sticks rather than bamboo if you can, taken from your garden or bought from a tree surgeon, as they'll blend more sympathetically into the background.

With tall plants, corral stems inside proprietary wire hoops and prop up smaller bushier plants with a ring of twiggy stems (known as pea sticks) pushed into the ground between plants. For creative ways to stake, *see* peony (page 98), delphinium (page 86) and sedum (page 142).

If plants flop before you have a chance to stake them, use two sticks pushed into the soil at angles to make a cross to prop them up as soon as possible, before their stems curve up to the light and can't be fixed.

KEEP A NOTEBOOK

Every gardener thinks they'll remember what they've planted and where. But inevitably some flowers get forgotten, especially bulbs and herbaceous plants that die down for part of the year, meaning they're at risk of being accidentally dug up or their

specific seasonal needs overlooked. Keep a notebook and record the names of plants you've bought and, even better, draw a map of exactly where they are. Labelling is a good idea, but the white plastic labels are too small for outdoors and are liable to break or get lost. Try cutting a bamboo cane to 20cm (8in) long instead, and inscribe the name of the plant on it with a permanent marker pen. It's visible without being conspicuous and lasts for ages outside in all weathers.

SPRING TRAMPLING

When you're working in borders, or have boisterous children and pets, it's all too easy for young shoots to be accidentally trampled. Particularly at risk are plants that are spindly or camouflaged against the soil, such as the young shoots of clematis, eremurus and lilies. With bulbs, all you need do to prevent a tragedy is place an upturned hanging basket over their crowns until they're large enough to spot. With clematis, a short length of drainage pipe to girdle the basal shoot will do the trick.

Cats are terrors for scratching in bare soil and will dislodge seedlings and small plants.

Stop the damage with twiggy branches snipped from hedges (but not thorns, which can stick in paws) and pushed into the soil around plants to discourage them.

COLD WEATHER

From autumn until spring extreme weather can strike in the shape of frosts, wild winds, torrential rain and hail. Tender plants and even hardy plants, if they're in pots, need protecting. For quick cover, drape horticultural fleece over the top of plants to insulate them from the worst of the weather. You might need to leave it on just for the night, or if the cold sets in, leave it on for a few days. Move containers of tender plants into a greenhouse or on to a cool windowsill indoors and hardy plants to a spot ideally next to your house walls in the warmth and shelter of the brickwork. Prevent compost from freezing by coddling the whole container in horticultural wrap. Cover half of the compost surface too, so pots don't become waterlogged by winter rain. Forewarned is forearmed, so if you have any tender plants, try to listen to the weather forecast. Take action fast.

CONTAINER PESTS

All container plants are at risk from a pest known as vine weevil. Look out for adult weevils in spring and autumn -- they're quite cheeky, sometimes even venturing into the house! They nibble the edges of leaves and lay eggs in pots, giving rise to voracious creamy coloured grubs with brown heads that gorge on roots. If a plant gets a bad attack, it looks as if it's wilting, but watering won't make any difference. The organic cure is to use nematodes – tiny worms that attack the grubs. Alternatively, use a chemical containing imidicloprid. Both are watered on to compost in spring and autumn as a preventative.

Sowing Plants from Seed

Sowing seed allows you to grow lots of plants that aren't available in the garden centre, for next to nothing. For most plants the ideal time to sow is in spring and the place to do it is in a greenhouse or indoors on a windowsill in 9cm (3in) pots filled with multipurpose or seed-sowing compost.

Once your teenaged plants have reached a reasonable size, it's time to plant them out.

1 Fill 8cm (3in) plastic pots loosely to the rim with compost and gently firm down with the base of another pot.
  Water the pots with a fine rose fitted to the spout of your watering can to avoid dislodging compost, and leave to drain for half an hour.

2 Sow seed thinly – roughly one seed per centimetre (½in) and move them around with your fingertip if they spill out in a pile. Sieve or sprinkle a thin layer of compost over the seed – unless it specifically says on the seed packet 'do not cover'. Then label.

3 Cover with a plastic cloche or with a plastic bag or place in a propagator to stop the compost drying out. Water with a spray mister if the top of the compost looks dry.

4 Replant when seedlings are 2.5cm (1in) tall and leaves are large enough to take between finger and thumb. Make holes in fresh pots or cell-trays of moist multipurpose compost with a short length of thin bamboo (or a pencil) and lower the seedling's roots into the hole. Plant the seedling at just below the height it was previously.

Ceanothus

Euphorbia

Cordyline

CHAPTER 2

Year-Round Structure

For year-round structure, you could pick almost any evergreen, but where you want, or already have, a distinctive style in your garden, what you need is a plant with personality, a real individual. If you're after a tropical look, then a Chusan palm or a giant bamboo will still say 'exotic' even when the summer flowers have gone to bed. That said, not all deciduous plants lose their character with their leaves. Dynamic willows and dogwoods can even look their best in winter.

Finally, there are the solid 'platoon' plants that can be used individually or in pairs – like lavender and box – to stand as evergreen sentinels, or lined up on parade for a more regimented formal look.

The sword-shaped foliage of phormium and whorled rosettes of euphorbia make a wonderful wintry, lead-green backdrop for corn-coloured stipa

Bamboo

Box

Bamboo

Everyone recognizes bamboo, but there are lots of different sorts – some with canes as tall as a house, some small and leafy – but all with hideously long Latin names! They have a reputation for taking over the garden with their spreading roots and thriving in damp ground, but this doesn't apply to any of the good garden varieties we've included. Bamboo are unfussy about soil and there are species for sun and full shade, but none can cope with a position in strong, drying winds, so always plant somewhere sheltered.

PROMOTE HEALTHY GROWTH

1 Mulch round the base with home-made compost or well-rotted manure in autumn to spur on lots of new shoots in spring.

2 With species that have attractive stems, like black bamboo, *Phyllostachys nigra*, prune off any lower branches that conceal the canes.

3 If growth starts to get very dense, remove old and dead canes at ground level in winter to show off the newer canes. Wear thick gloves to protect your hands from the sharp stumps. Then mulch to give the plant a boost.

4 When bamboo grown in containers become pot-bound, knock out the plant in winter (before growth starts) and divide the roots. You'll need a bowsaw as they're that tough!

5 Few species need pruning, but *Pleioblastus*, which is grown for its variegated leaves rather than its canes, can be cut down to the base in late winter to encourage lots of new leaves.

28

PICK THE BEST FOR YOUR GARDEN

• *Thamnocalamus crassinodus* 'Kew Beauty' – A well-behaved clump-former with red-tipped canes covered in a ghostly blue bloom of leaves.
H 4m (12ft)

• *Phyllostachys nigra* – A clump-forming bamboo with black canes.
H&S 250x75cm (8x2½ft)

• *Phyllostachys aurea* – A golden-caned clump-former.
H&S 2.5x3.5m (8x2ft)

• *Pleioblastus auricomus* – This has golden-variegated leaves, grows well in a container and is ideal for sun.
H 1m (3ft)

• *Fargesia murielae* – This leafy, graceful bamboo has pencil-thick grey-green canes.
H 2.5m (8ft)

Phyllostachys vivax – for golden canes as thick as your wrist

PLANT IN POTS

Bamboo are easy to grow and look brilliant in pots; this is also a great way to contain small, spreading types such as the variegated *Pleioblastus auricomus* and *P. variegatus*.

Pot into a mix of loam-based John Innes No.2 with some finely composted bark mixed in. Avoid 'Ali Baba'-shaped pots (with an incurving rim) as it'll be impossible to repot the plant without smashing the container – traditional vase shapes are best. Water regularly through the summer and feed in autumn with bonemeal.

TIP

Pruned bamboo canes can be used along edges of paths or lawns to hold back sprawling stems by creating a hoop

Sweet Bay

If it's an evergreen pot plant you want, buy sweet bay (*Laurus nobilis*). Not only is it a cooking herb, you can buy them pre-shaped into lollipops and pyramids, adding style to cottage, formal or contemporary gardens. Bay can survive in a pot for years if you remember to water it regularly. Pinch the occasional leaf to spice up pork roasts and salmon, or for tossing on the barbecue to add that sweet smoky taste to burgers. Be careful not to use cherry laurel (*Prunus laurocerasus*), which looks almost identical but which is not edible.

POTTING UP YOUR TREE

1 Pot up your bay tree for instant height and impact. The container should be at least 45cm (18in) wide to give roots room and prevent it blowing over. Use a loam-based John Innes No.3 compost mixed with peat-free multipurpose and place the container in a sunny spot.

2 To keep the shape, use secateurs to take off individual leaves in late spring and late summer (don't use shears – they butcher leaves) and snip off any with brown leaf tips caused by bad weather at the same time.

3 Feed every spring with a slow-release fertilizer and every couple of years, freshen up the soil by tipping the pot on its side, scraping away the top few inches of soil and replacing with fresh John Innes No.3.

PESTS

WATCH OUT FOR SOOTY LEAVES

If leaves curl up, become pale or marked with sooty black markings, the culprit is bay sucker, a sap-sucking scale insect. Check undersides of leaves for a small brown bug that looks a bit like a split lentil. It's hard to get rid of, but it's worth trying the organic method using nematodes (tiny parasitic worms) in late spring before the young insects are on the move.

HEIGHT & SPREAD 1.5mx80cm (5x3ft), but twice the size if left unclipped CLIMATE ZONE 9

A lollipop bay in a pot makes a fine centrepiece for a round cut-flower garden

4 City and coastal gardeners can get away with planting bay trees (they're salt tolerant) in a border, but for cooler gardens grow in a pot that can be moved into shelter during winter. A porch or even the lee of a warm wall is just the spot to keep it safe and snug.

Bay combines the best of Mediterranean formality and practicality, with their topiary shape and edible leaves.

Box

A classic evergreen, box (*Buxus sempervirens*) is the plant for topiary and low hedges. Left to grow unchecked, it's unremarkable, but clipped once or twice a year, it brings evergreen shape to your garden making a perfect foil for flowers. It's very versatile too, coping in full shade and full sun. It'll grow in any ordinary soil except waterlogged.

Nowadays, you can buy large ready-clipped topiary box, but these can be expensive. For economy, where you need lots of plants for hedges, buy small plants or grow from cuttings.

GROW IN THE GROUND

1 Soak pots well before planting – this is really important because the fibrous roots pack the pots and make it hard to wet. Plant in soil that has been enriched with some compost, at the same level it was in the pot. Design-wise, box looks best on the ends and corners of borders, to give winter structure and a background for border plants. Alternatively, use as sentinels either side of the end of a path. Space hedging plants 30cm (12in) apart – the best time to plant is autumn.

2 Keep box plants watered in hot weather for the first year and clip twice a year in late spring and late summer. With cones and pyramids, place a tee-pee of bamboo canes over the plant to give you a straight line to cut to. You will find it easier when clipping around curves to turn the shears upside down.

3 In small gardens or on gravel, where it is more awkward to clear up, place newspaper at the foot of the plants to catch the clippings as you cut.

Have fun with box hedges and clip portions into eccentric shapes, like this teardrop (FAR RIGHT)

HEIGHT & SPREAD 30x120cm (1x4ft) grown as a hedge; topiary up to 180cm (6ft) CLIMATE ZONE 5

GROW IN POTS

The best compost is a half-and-half mix of multipurpose and loam-based John Innes No.3. Water the plant regularly through the growing season and feed once a month with a balanced liquid fertilizer.

Turning the pot occasionally will ensure that all sides get plenty of light and grow evenly.

Box trees were born to flatter – their shapes and **evergreen** colour are guaranteed to make other plants **look good.**

TIPS

TAKE CUTTINGS

Cuttings are easy to root and late autumn is the time to do it. Cut 10cm (4in) lengths from the tips of plants and remove the leaves from the lower half. Push into pots of half-and-half multipurpose and horticultural grit. Keep them outside or in a cold glasshouse through winter, and they'll root away ready for potting up in spring.

Cordyline and Phormium

It's hard to tell the difference between these two shrubs at the garden centre, even though they grow to look quite different over time. Cordyline lives up to its common name (cabbage palm) and develops a trunk, while phormium (New Zealand flax) slowly spreads into an arching clump. Both are architectural foliage plants, bestowing an exotic feel to a garden. They cope well in salt-sprayed coastal gardens, preferring well-drained soil and lots of sun; if your soil is heavy, add plenty of organic matter and grit when planting, or plant in containers for instant drama.

CORDYLINE

The hardiest cordyline is olive-green *C. australis*, but if your garden rarely dips below freezing, you can get away with the more striking purple or green-striped varieties. That said, *C. australis* is more likely to produce a trunk and, in a sheltered garden, can make palm-like trees 4m (13ft) tall and even produce clusters of sweetly scented flowers.

1 Remove lower leaves as they turn yellow and tatty. Cut as close to the stem as possible to leave a neat finish.

2 If prolonged wet, cold winter weather is forecast, gather the foliage together in the centre and tie it with twine to protect the growing point at the centre of the rosette from rot.

Potted cordyline (LEFT); **planting phormium** (RIGHT); a phormium provides striking and dramatic evergreen structure to any border (FAR RIGHT)

HEIGHT & SPREAD 4x2m (13x7ft) CLIMATE ZONE 9

PHORMIUM

More variable than cordyline, phormium come in a range of yellows, pinks, purples, bronze and greens. The largest is *Phormium tenax*, which grows into a 3m (10ft) monster with pointed leaves arranged like a giant Indian head-dress. Its vigour enables it to cope even in quite shady gardens. *P. cookianum* is smaller and has a softer look with long, gracefully arching leaves. 'Maori Sunrise' and 'Sundowner' have pink margins to the leaves which pick up the colours of neighbouring flowers and contrast well with green and silver foliage.

WHERE TO PLANT

Plant in spring where their full shape can be seen, such as on the corners of borders or as a focal point at the end of a path. If you like the tropical look, use phormium as an evergreen backbone in borders, or for a contemporary urban look combine with pebbles, gravel or decking.

Phormium look fantastic back-lit, so plant where the evening sun catches the leaves to give a fiery glow.

Willow and Dogwood

Most plants are grown for flowers or foliage but dogwoods (*Cornus*) and willows (*Salix*) are invaluable for their vibrant winter stems. They come in colours from black, green and red through to purple and fiery orange. They love boggy ground but will grow in drier soil, just not so vigorously. They make wonderful hedges to attract wildlife, too. Both will form trees, but if you chop them back every two to three years, they will keep to a manageable size. The useful stems can be cut for making stakes, winter flower arrangements and even garden seats.

GROW IN A BORDER

The most ornamental dogwoods for borders are the luminous 'Midwinter Fire' or the crimson-stemmed 'Elegantissima' with its variegated leaves. Ideally plant where the low winter sun catches the stems. Mulch every autumn to create a dark foil for the stems, then every two years, prune stems right down to the ground in spring before growth starts.

MAKE YOUR OWN GARDEN STAKES

If you have a wild corner at the bottom of your garden around 1.5x1.5m (5x5ft), you can grow two or three willows for harvesting to make stakes or baskets. Choose a mixture of varieties for different coloured stems. Try olive-green-stemmed *Salix viminalis*, orange *S. alba* subsp. *vitellina* 'Britzensis' and purple *S. daphnoides* 'Aglaia'.

Here's how to make the garden stake used with delphiniums on page 86.

2 Push straight lengths through the outside of the hoop to make a cross.

1 Plait pencil-thin stems together to make a hoop and secure them with twine.

3 Finally, push the hoop down on to three bamboo canes around the plant to be supported.

Dogwood gives you flowers and berries, as well as fiery winter stems (ABOVE AND RIGHT)

GROW A WILDLIFE HEDGE

The best variety to create a hedge for wildlife is common dogwood, *Cornus alba*, which has blood-red winter bark, white flowers in late spring and white fruits in autumn. Plant in autumn and mix with other native trees, such as hawthorn, elder, beech and hazel. Plant daffodils along the base for extra colour in early spring.

CUTTINGS FROM PRUNINGS

There's nothing fiddly about taking willow and dogwood cuttings. Trim pencil-thin lengths with secateurs in winter and push them straight into the ground. They'll root away and leaf up in spring. Wait until autumn when you can dig them up with a spade and plant where you want them to grow. Alternatively, if you have bare ground, strike lots of willow wands 15cm (6in) apart to make a living willow fence.

Dogwoods are best for smaller gardens, but both dogwood and willow can be kept to a manageable size through regular cutting down.

Euphorbia

Look in the euphorbia section at the garden centre and you'll find dozens of good plants, suitable for most parts of the garden from the cool, shady side to the hottest alpine scree. They all have a long season of interest, many are evergreen and are very striking plants that beautifully complement almost any other plants you put them with. This selection do well in all garden soils except boggy ground. Even better, they're almost maintenance free!

PICK THE RIGHT PLANT FOR THE RIGHT PLACE

FOR A HOT, DRY SPOT

Great for breaking up expanses of gravel and in easy-care pots, *Euphorbia myrsinites* looks like a succulent with evergreen leaves and snaking stems that hug the ground. Also good for the front of a tropical-style border. Cut back the flowered stems to the base when they finish.
H&S 15x30cm (6x12in)

FOR A TROPICAL LOOK

Euphorbia mellifera has the most attractive foliage of all with long, elegant leaves and honey-scented flowers in late spring. Though it's got a reputation for being tender, it's hardier than many people give it credit for. A young plant survived uncovered in our garden down to –6°C (21°F), so it's worth a go in most gardens and it grows in dappled shade, though it's less likely to flower. Pruning is unnecessary although you might want to deadhead it after flowering.
H&S 120x120cm (4x4ft)

FOR DEEP SHADE

Euphorbia amygdaloides var. *robbiae* is a tough, spreading woodlander that copes in poor, dry soils even under trees and on banks. Its leaves are held in rosettes, topped by lime-green sprays of flowers in spring that look fabulous with daffodils and bluebells, and can even make a forsythia look special. The spent flowers burnish through summer, so wait until winter before cutting them back to the leaves and take out dead stems too. H: 60cm (2ft)
For red-tinted foliage, try *E. amygdaloides* 'Rubra'.
H&S 30x30cm (1x1ft)

Who'd have thought a plant with green **flowers** would be so **valuable** in the garden? Euphorbia gives you evergreen shape and texture too!

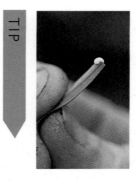

BACK OF THE BORDER

The appeal of *Euphorbia characias* is that it changes colour to suit the season. In spring its leaves are fresh-green with a zesty mint-chocolate look, then from summer onwards the foliage becomes blue. It's the ideal backdrop for red hot pokers and the oatmeal shades of ornamental grasses. Cut down the dead flower-stems at the base with secateurs, leaving just the stems that haven't yet flowered in place.
H&S 120x90cm (4x3ft)

SPICY SPRING COLOUR

Euphorbia 'Fireglow' is another good choice for a tropical-style border. It is deciduous with spreading stems that emerge, as if on fire, with the daffodils. They hold their colour well into autumn and are topped with orange flower-bracts. Although a spreader it's not invasive and it has an airy feel that won't shade out neighbours. Plant in well-drained soil in sun or part-shade with grasses and salvia.
H&S 90x60cm (3x2ft)

TIP

TAKE CARE WITH SAP

All euphorbia exude a milky white sap when the stems and leaves are broken which can burn the skin, particularly on sunny days.

Take a commonsense approach when planting. Don't position next to paths where they'll be brushed by; if you have children that play in the garden, keep the plants tucked towards the back of the border. Always wear gloves when you are cutting stems and when taking cuttings.

Japanese Maple

The joy of a Japanese maple (*Acer palmatum*) is the stunning foliage as it emerges in spring and again when it tints in autumn. While they're no harder to grow than any other tree, their beautiful leaves need protecting from leaf-scorching winds and frosts in early spring. One way is to plant under the airy canopy of a larger tree. Alternatively grow in a container that you can move to shelter as leaves are emerging. Once leaves have fully emerged, maples are less delicate and can happily sit on the patio's cool side.

GROW IN A POT

1 Buy a 30–45cm (12–18in) pot with holes in the base. Cover the holes with crocks or broken polystyrene to prevent soil from being washed out, but still allow for drainage.

2 Mix half-and-half peat-free multipurpose compost with a loam-based John Innes No.3.

3 Upend the pot and knock the rootball out of its container by tapping the rim against the heel of your palm, taking care not to damage the branches.

TIP

TRAIN THE BRANCHES

Acer palmatum dissectum is slow-growing and has a natural oriental look that's tiered and weeping. This can be enhanced by training any crossing or oddly placed branches with twine to make the tree perfectly balanced. Loop the twine between the branch and the main trunk, gently pulling it as closely as possible to the position you want. After a month or so, twine can be removed as the branch will have set in its new position.

The newest leaves on the branch-tips are the brightest, highlighting the deeper bronze of the older foliage

HEIGHT & SPREAD 120x120cm (4x4ft) CLIMATE ZONES 6–9

Acer palmatum dissectum
'Inaba-shidare' tints a beautiful
crimson in autumn.

4 Cover the base of the pot with compost until it brings the height of the maple to 2.5–5cm (1–2in) below the rim. This will allow for easy watering and less will run off from the top. Back-fill around the roots with compost, pressing down firmly around the sides to remove air pockets.

5 For an authentic Japanese garden feel, dress the top of the compost with moss raked from your lawn or gathered from guttering. Keep well watered and feed once a month through the growing season with a balanced liquid fertilizer. Keep a look-out for aphids and then spray with organic insecticide if necessary.

Lavender

Everyone loves lavender (*Lavandula*) and knows it's easy to grow, but for plants to look their best and live a long time, there are a few essentials. First, if you have heavy clay soil, be prepared to improve drainage either by making raised beds, or by digging in bucketfuls of grit. In sandy and sun-filled gardens, your lavender could live for 20 years or more!
To find out how to grow a lavender hedge, head to page 50.

KEEP IT LOOKING GOOD

1 Plant containerized lavender in spring, or bare-root plants in late autumn. Always plant in full sun, otherwise it will sprawl towards the light and become lopsided. In late summer, prune off the dead flower-spikes with shears, going back to 2.5cm (1in) below where the flower emerges, and no harder.

2 In spring just as growth starts, cut into a 20cm (8in) hummock with secateurs.

3 *Lavandula angustifolia* and its varieties can be pruned hard back if they become leggy, but never hard prune French lavender, *L. stoechas* or *L.* x *intermedia*.

4 Unlike English lavender (above), prune French lavender by dead-heading through summer and trimming in autumn when it's finished.

WHAT TO USE WHERE

There are many different varieties of lavender, some dwarf, some variegated, others that have leaves with a high oil content which are good for herbal use.

● **Draping over walls** – *Lavandula angustifolia* 'Munstead' makes a low cushion of dense foliage with bluer flowers in midsummer.
H&S 60x30cm (2x1ft)

● **Windowboxes and hanging baskets** – *L. a.* 'Little Lottie' forms lilac-pink domed bushes.
H&S 40x20cm (15x9in)

● **Best flowers** – *L. stoechas pedunculata*, the French Lavender, has the prettiest flowers topped with dark purple petals that flutter with the breeze.
H&S 50x50cm (20x20in)

● **Herb garden/sachets** – *L. a.* 'Royal Purple' has long-stalked deep purple flowers for drying and potpourri.
H&S 60x60cm (24x24in)

The flower-spikes of French lavender are topped by a plum-purple head-dress (RIGHT AND BELOW)

Lavender is the ultimate sun-worshipper – at its most oily and aromatic in the hottest parts of the day.

PESTS

CATS AND DOGS

If your lavender suddenly turns black with no apparent explanation, the reason is almost certainly that cats or dogs have been using it as a toilet. Beware, just one tinkle can kill a plant overnight.

With lavender in large pots and half-barrels, lay a piece of mesh around the plant and fix into the rim, then cover it with pebbles to discourage cats from scratching around in the soil.

Ceanothus

There aren't very many blue-flowered shrubs and certainly not many as early in the year as ceanothus (California lilac). *Ceanothus* 'Puget Blue' is the hardiest of the evergreens and has neat, dark-green, glossy leaves. It flowers for a few weeks in late spring and is smothered in small pompoms. Its silvery leaves are a good foil for 'hot' schemes and, though not a true climber, is brilliant for cladding walls quickly as it grows fast without getting into your guttering. It also copes with salty coastal winds and bees love it too.

GROW AND TRAIN CEANOTHUS

1 Plant in improved soil 45cm (18in) away from the house wall, tilting the plant back towards the house. Put up wires at 45cm (18in) intervals held off the wall by vine eyes – wall screws with eye holes.

2 After flowering is the time to prune. It's not essential but may be necessary if stems are interfering with windows or straying too far forwards into the border. You can prune as much as two-thirds off each new shoot, but never into old wood. Be careful though – the more you prune, the greater the likelihood you'll lose some of next year's flowers.

3 Plants grow so fast that training is essential to keep them flat against the wall.

Use horticultural twine to pull individual stems back to wires, fanning out the stems into an attractive shape. Because you're letting more light get to the stems, more leaves grow and this helps to stop the ceanothus looking bare at the base.

Ceanothus 'Puget Blue' becomes a puffball of blue flowers in spring
(RIGHT AND FAR RIGHT)

HEIGHT & SPREAD 2.5x2.5m (9x9ft) CLIMATE ZONE 8

Want to **cover** a warm house wall **fast**? Then ceanothus is your **plant**!

TIP

LIVE FAST, DIE YOUNG
The only downside of ceanothus is that it's not long-lived. Anything over ten years is a good run. Don't struggle on with plants that are showing their age, instead dig them up and plant a fresh young thing. Within two summers it will be almost as big. For an extra season of interest from mid to late summer, train a *Clematis viticella* through the leaves and should the base go bare, hide it with silver evergreens, like *Artemisia* 'Powis Castle' (*see page 126*) or Dutch lavender (*L. x intermedia*) (*see page 51*).

Chusan Palm

You can't get more 'tropical island' than a palm, and the hardiest is the Chusan (*Trachycarpus fortunei*) which survives temperatures down to −10°C (14°F). It has fan-shaped, evergreen leaves and a trunk as furry as an orang-outang. For a price, you can buy plants up to 6m (19ft) tall and though costly, the larger the plant, the more reliably hardy it will be. If you're on a budget, buy a small one that hasn't yet formed a trunk, plant it in a container and keep in a sheltered spot while young.

HOW TO PLANT YOUR PALM

2 In spring, feed with a slow-release balanced fertilizer to fuel the production of new leaves and, as an extra pick-me-up, water with a seaweed solution from the garden centre at the same time. It's one of the fastest ways to put colour back into wan leaves.

3 As older leaves deteriorate with time, trim them off right back to the trunk. This won't affect the growth of the plant as all fresh leaves emerge from the crown at the top in the centre.

1 Choose a sunny spot out of the wind – wind turns leaf tips brown and yellows the foliage. If your soil is heavy, improve it with bark, grit and compost and if it has a lot of clay, consider planting in a large pot. Stake any tree with a stem taller than 90cm (3ft) to stop wind rock damaging roots. The stake can be removed after a couple of years.

4 In winter, if extremely cold weather is forecast, wrap the growing tip at the crown with horticultural fleece, and for plants in pots, coddle the whole container in bubble-wrap to stop roots freezing.

HEIGHT & SPREAD H 2m (6ft) a decade, S 1m (3ft) maximum at ground level CLIMATE ZONES 9–11

The **best** hardy **exotic** for busy gardeners, the **Chusan** palm is **evergreen** and self-sufficient.

LIGHT IT UP AT NIGHT
Because the leaf silhouettes are so strong, palms are great subjects for lighting and casting exotic shadows over your patio. The Chusan is so versatile, you can uplight it with spotlamps to show off the trunk and leaves; downlight with wall-mounted lights to cast patterns on the floor or backlight to highlight the spiky outline. It'll create a funky, urban feel whatever the season.

Day or night, Chusan palm leaves make strong silhouettes

Tree Fern

Think of a fern and you might imagine something delicate and leafy, but tree ferns (*Dicksonia antarctica*) are huge! Like palms and bamboo, just one plant is sufficient to give a place a changed feel – in this case ancient and ethereal. Trickier to grow than palms and bamboo, though, the tree fern dislikes severe cold and can't abide dryness but it loves the warm drizzle of its native Tasmania. Replicate this and you'll make them feel at home.

CARE FOR YOUR FERN

1 Plant in the shade in spring, ideally in the dappled shelter of trees, adding lots of compost and leafmould to the soil at the same time. Tree ferns are available pot grown or as trunks that re-sprout from the top. Plant trunks by setting their base 10cm (4in) deep into the soil and, because all tree ferns are shallow-rooted, lash to a sturdy stake, hidden from view at the back.

2 The growing point is in the crown – in the top of the trunk – and this is where you should water. The surest way (and safest for what is an expensive plant!) is to attach it to automatic irrigation. A container-garden kit is simplest, ideally with an automatic timer set to come on a few times a day through the growing season to keep the trunk wet at all times. If you can't do this, give it a spray with the hose once a day. For plentiful fronds, some nurseries recommend feeding with a dilute liquid fertilizer directly into the crown once a month through summer.

3 In colder areas where frosts are frequent, protect the growing point by wrapping in horticultural fleece or straw until early spring.

TIP

Buy the biggest tree fern you can afford. It will be expensive but less likely to suffer in a hard winter – the thicker the trunk, the greater the insulation. Unfurling leaves are prone to twisting when being moved from the nursery, so if you grow it in a pot, don't move it when fronds are unfurling.

HEIGHT & SPREAD 3.5x3.5m (10x10ft) CLIMATE ZONE 6

This is Jurassic Park for real – tree ferns have been around since the time of the dinosaurs!

Plant a Lavender Hedge

A lavender hedge can be snaking and informal or mirrored either side of a path. It never gets too big and is incredibly romantic, with silver foliage and fragrant summer flowers. It has the abundant feel of a crop, and because there are so many flowers there will always be enough sprigs to cut for the house. Although it doesn't have the dense winter foliage of other evergreens, what it lacks in the coldest part of the year it more than makes up for when the hot weather arrives.

HOW TO PLANT

1 Dig out a trench along the line where you want your hedge, roughly 30cm (1ft) deep and wide. If your soil is clay, pour in grit along its length, around half a bucket for every plant.

2 Fork over the bottom of the trench, adding compost if the soil has never been previously cultivated, and mix in grit if your soil is heavy.

3 Set plants in position along the base of the trench, spacing them 30cm (12in) apart. Make sure the plants are level as you go and add or remove soil as necessary.

4 Knock the plants out of their pots, replace in the trench, then shovel in soil on either side of the row.

5 Firm around each plant with your fingers, levelling off the soil as you go.

6 Water plants in well to settle the soil. Add spring colour by planting *Anemone blanda* alongside and buy purple violas in autumn for winter colour.

BEST VARIETIES FOR HEDGES

• *Lavendula angustifolia* 'Imperial Gem' – Similar to classic 'Hidcote' but compact and producing more intense flowers.
H&S 50x50cm (20x20in)

• *L. a.* 'Hidcote' – A classic variety for hedges with violet flower-spikes in midsummer.
H&S 60x50cm (24x20in)

• *L. a.* 'Sawyers' – The dusty-grey foliage keeps its silvery tones well in winter; it has pale purple flowers with a blue centre in midsummer.
H&S 50x50cm (20x20in)

• Dutch lavender (*L. x intermedia* Dutch Group, also called 'Vera') – These very large, robust plants have blue flowers from mid- to late summer.
H&S 120x90cm (4x3ft)

Hedges crop abundant flowers, so you need never feel guilty about stealing bundles for the house

TIP

IF ONE PLANT DIES …
Filling gaps in lavender hedges is difficult as the oils in their foliage contain growth retardants to stop new plants establishing amongst them. Overcome this by clipping plants back hard either side of the gap in winter, to concentrate their efforts on re-growth and not compromising their neighbour.

Bearded Iris

Tulip

Canna

Allium

CHAPTER 3

Flowers with Impact

At any successful party the guest list should always include one or two larger-than-life characters who will add a bit of fun and glamour. It's the same with gardens – they can be a bit tame without one or two extroverts.

By nature, impact flowers have eye-catching shapes that make them stand out from the crowd. Use these bold beauties as stand-alone plants to rise above the rest or be clever and match their shades with existing flowers and discover how brilliantly they can emphasize the colour scheme.

Many of this selection are bulbs, so they're perfect for cramming in between other plants even if your borders are already fairly full, so there's every excuse to overindulge!

Eremurus (foxtail lilies) are horticultural dynamite, their taper-like flowers go off in succession, fizzling up from the base, as if someone's put a match to the fuse. Here they rise above a crowd of scarlet California poppies

Drumstick Allium

Allium are distinctive because they are spherical – you don't get many round flowers – and their colour is outstanding. For that designer look, plant bulbs by the dozen and choose the most dramatic drumsticks, like *Allium* 'Globemaster' and 'Purple Sensation'. Position near the front of the border where spring leaves will get plenty of sun, but will be covered by low foliage of neighbours as they retreat in summer. Allium are easy to grow, coming up year after year, but dislike boggy soils.

PLANTING ALLIUM BULBS

1 Look out for bulbs at late summer shows and at garden centres. In early autumn, plant 7.5cm (3in) deep, no closer than 30cm (1ft) apart in sun. If you miss the boat, buy pot plants in spring, but they're more expensive this way. Because leaves emerge early they're vulnerable to slug attack so put out preventative traps or wildlife-friendly slug pellets.

2 Design-wise, think of allium as an extra layer of flowers above what's already in your early summer borders, and grow low sprawlers, like hardy geranium, silver-leaved artemisia and sage between them.

3 Allium are two-seasonal, as the flowers dry to sun-bleached stars in autumn, stunning with grasses and rudbeckia and a reminder to plant more! In wet years they spoil, so cut and bring them indoors for vases.

This **designer** bulb has been **fashionable** for years – nothing else can **touch it** for early-summer **shape** and colour.

TIP

MARK THE
PLANTING SPOT

You always think you'll remember where bulbs are planted but you never do, so avoid the anguish of accidentally spearing or digging up hidden bulbs, and place a pebble on top to mark the planting spots.

Allium 'Purple Sensation'

African Lily

The African lily (*Agapanthus*) has a reputation for being tender and therefore delicate but these days most commonly available varieties, including the well-known Headbourne hybrids, are hardy and content in any free-draining soil. They're best though in pots where their lofty blue tubular flowers are more upstanding and echo the brilliant blue summer skies. The African lily with most impact is the old tender variety *Agapanthus africanus*. It has the best leaves of all, thick, lush and evergreen, and the flowers teeter over 1m (4ft) above them.

GROW IN A POT

1 Choose a terracotta pot only slightly larger than the container the plant came in, as having congested roots encourages flowers. Put a 2–3cm (1in) layer of crocks or gravel in the base to enable excess water to drain out of the pot.

2 The roots are fleshy and cling to the side of the pot, so it's easiest to get the plant out of the pot by turning it upside down and tapping the rim on the edge of a table.

3 Plant using a mix of two-thirds soil-based John Innes No.2 and one-third composted bark and use a thin length of wood to gently firm soil around roots, to ensure there are no air pockets. Leave a 2cm (1in) gap between the top of the compost and the rim to aid watering.

TIPS

PLANT A POT WITHIN A POT

African lilies are one of the few plants that can sit on their own in a classical urn and look good for most of the summer. The trick is to plunge them while still in their pot into the urn, then pack it round with compost or pebbles to hold it in place. This technique keeps the roots of the lily congested, so the flowers keep coming, and means you can easily remove and store the plant in winter, without having to move the heavy urn. Instead it can be filled with violas for colour during the colder months.

HEIGHT & SPREAD 70–120cm (16–48in) x 70cm (16in) CLIMATE ZONES 9–10

4 Water regularly and once a week throughout summer add a dilute tomato feed that's high in potash to the watering can and deadhead flowers to the base as they die off.

5 Before the frosts, move all pots, even hardy varieties, close to the house where they're less likely to get waterlogged and the pots damaged by frost. Move tender types to a conservatory or a frost-free greenhouse and keep on the dry side – watch out for mealy bug and red spider mites through winter.

The tender but gorgeous *Agapanthus africanus*

African lilies are the connoisseur container plant for retro colonial style – stunning in huge stone urns and large terracotta planters.

Foxtail Lily

Beware the foxtail lily (*Eremurus*) – it can turn you into a gardening geek, telling anyone who'll listen about its mythically proportioned flower-spikes and the horticultural heroics required to grow it.

You may love it but you mustn't crowd it. Ultimately it's a loner that needs a space all of its own to produce those covetable sky-high spires.

GROWING FROM CROWNS

1 Buy crowns from the bulb section or, for better choice and quality, from a specialist nursery in autumn or early spring. Plant in sun, 15cm (6in) deep and 60–90cm (2–3ft) apart, fanning out the spidery roots on a mound of soil in a hole wide enough to take their spread.

2 When foliage appears, use an upturned hanging basket or pebbles to prevent accidental trampling and protect from slugs with organic pellets. In early summer when it starts the sprint towards flowering, it will need water if it doesn't rain for more than a fortnight.

3 Once foxtail lilies go to seed and the pea-like pods appear, stop watering, cut the stems back to the base and allow foliage to wither away naturally. Don't cover that ugly withering foliage with anything that needs watering, as the roots need to dry off in the soil.

TIP

GIVE IT THE RIGHT SOIL ...

If you buy a pot-grown foxtail lily, you may be fooled into thinking they flower easily, but it's the following summer that they may disappoint. Their desert ancestry means they like baking summers and chilly, dry winters. So, when planting, improve the soil drainage by adding half a bucket of horticultural grit. If your soil has a lot of clay in it, pile the soil into a mound (*see* page 15) to keep crowns dry in winter.

Foxtail lilies are like horticultural **fireworks** – half the fun is in the **suspense**, as the spikes soar.

Eremurus robustus (ABOVE)
Eremurus stenophyllus (RIGHT)

BEST CHOICE

Our favourites are:

• The pale-peach *Eremurus robustus*. H 180cm (6ft)

• The Ruiters hybrid 'Pinocchio' is smaller and has cinnamon blooms. H 90–120cm (3–4ft)

• For lime-yellow flowers try *E. stenophyllus*. H 120–180cm (4–6ft) These contrast well with 'Arabian Night' dahlias which are ideal because they do not shade the eremurus foliage until it dies off.

Bearded Iris

Bearded iris bloom in late spring and early summer, and add glamour to all the natural-looking early summer flowers. If you want an undemanding type, grow *Iris germanica* – it has lemon or rich purple and lavender, scented flowers and grows happily without fuss, provided it has well-drained soil and full sun. It's one of the many forefathers of modern hybrid varieties that come in stunning colours and ruffles, like puffed-up birds of paradise. But beware, the more extraordinary the flower, the greater the likelihood that it will be a primadonna, tending to be smaller and less vigorous than the blue and yellow types.

HOW TO GROW

1 Iris prefer alkaline conditions so chalk or lime soils are best (basically where rhododendrons don't grow). Improve soil with mushroom compost before planting. Give them a spot out in the open, at the front of the border or in a gravel garden, as they hate to be crowded. If the soil is heavy add grit to the planting hole too. When planting, plant no deeper than it was in its pot, so the top of the rhizome (the fleshy ginger-like root) is left unburied and exposed to the sun.

2 Flowers are spectacular but fleeting, so deadhead each one by pinching out the bloom between finger and thumb as they die off to keep the plant looking good.

3 Every three years, divide and replant the rhizomes after flowering, or in autumn. Replant only the plumpest, youngest portion (these won't have old flower spikes on them) and discard the oldest, shrivelled portions.

HEIGHT & SPREAD 90x50cm (36x30in) CLIMATE ZONES 5–8

Irises are the first act of **summer**, they come into flower like a troop of **exotic** can-can dancers, **waving** their petticoats to the **world**.

Lemon bearded iris

4 Cut down the leaves to 20cm (8in) to prevent plants being wind-rocked. Some people find the sap of iris irritating so if you have sensitive skin, wear gloves when handling.

TIP

PLANT IN A CIRCLE

If you have enough plants, bearded iris always look very effective planted in a circle as this emulates how they grow naturally. Point rhizomes into the centre like the hands of a clock. This way you get a nice big clump of flowers without crowding the roots.

Foxglove

The flowers for fairy hats and foxes' mittens, foxgloves (*Digitalis*) add bags of bee-buzzing, cottage charm. Each plant makes a single spike of purple, white or apricot bells, so you need a good few for a woodland look. The best way to get lots of plants is to sow a packet of seed, then plant them out in groups to flower in early summer. Although biennial, from just one sowing, they'll go native and spread around naturally if you're careful with your weeding.

GROW FOXGLOVES FROM SEED

1 Sow seed of *Digitalis purpurea* or 'Excelsior Hybrids' in summer and when seedlings come up, move each one into its own 7.5cm (3in) pot of multipurpose compost and store in a greenhouse, coldframe or just somewhere out of the way and sheltered outdoors (*see* page 24 for how to sow seeds in pots).

2 If you can, plant out in autumn so they'll have the last dregs of summer to clump up into luscious flowering plants for next year. If your borders are so crammed with plants there's no room, pot them on again until spaces appear in autumn.

3 Until you get round to planting, keep the plants watered and fed with a half-strength liquid feed of balanced fertilizer – you can tell when they're hungry as the leaves go light green.

PERENNIAL FOXGLOVES TO TRY

If you don't want to sow seed, buy foxgloves as plants. The best are the later-flowering *Digitalis ferruginea*, which has rusty-coloured flowers that dry to make good winter skeletons, or *Digitalis* x *mertonensis*, which is pretty but precious – happy one minute and dead the next! Another one to consider is the butter-yellow *Digitalis grandiflora*.

HEIGHT & SPREAD 150x30cm (5x1ft) CLIMATE ZONE 5

Wild white and purple foxgloves have flowers on just one side of the stem and thrive in dry shade or sun

4 Plant out in patches of three or five – beside roses in sun (provided soil is moist) or with hostas and ferns in shade. Odd numbers always look more natural. Foxgloves like a woodland soil, rich in organic matter, so add lots of leafmould and compost when planting.

Wherever there's a foxglove flowering, there's sure to be a bee frantically buzzing in and out of its beautiful purple blooms.

Lily

If you like to sit out in the evening, you can't beat lilies (*Lilium*) for night-time scent and impact. Of the many types on offer, the tallest and most striking are the oriental and trumpet varieties, such as the classic scented 'Stargazer' and regal lily (*Lilium regale*). Buy either from a mail order specialist or choose plump, mould-free bulbs from a garden centre in early autumn for the pick of the crop and flowers in late summer. Plant as soon as you get them home. Alternatively buy and plant them in spring, but expect flowers later in summer.

START LILIES FROM BULBS

1 Trowel out a hole 15cm (6in) deep, sprinkle some grit in the base and set the bulb on its side in the hole to prevent water collecting between the scales.

2 Fill over with soil and put a pebble on top so you don't accidentally dig it up before it grows! For a natural look, plant in drifts among roses and ornamental grasses, leaving about 60cm (2ft) between bulbs.

PESTS

WHAT TO WATCH OUT FOR
The first sign this shiny red lily beetle and its offspring are at work are shredded leaves, occurring any time from spring until autumn. Because they can ruin a plant in just a few days, you need to act fast by picking off beetles and squashing. Do it carefully because they sense motion and drop off the plant and hide. Look out for and scrape off larvae at the same time – they look like bird droppings found on the underside or on top of leaves.

Trumpet lilies, like night-scented 'African Queen', are tall and flower throughout summer (RIGHT)

HEIGHT & SPREAD 120x30cm (4x1ft) CLIMATE ZONES 5–6

The **tallest** and most **striking** lilies are the **oriental** and **trumpet** varieties.

KEEP THEM FLOWERING

An old florist's trick to keep lilies flowering longer is to pinch out the stamens. This also stops you getting covered in clothes-staining pollen when weeding! To encourage a good flush of flowers next summer, cut off the seed-pods (ABOVE) and sprinkle a general fertilizer around the base.

Tulip

If you haven't grown tulips (*Tulipa*) before, give them a go – they're guaranteed to come up next spring. After that, it's down to your soil and how much trouble you go to if you want to keep them for years. On light well-drained soils, they look after themselves, so you can plant bulbs through emerging herbaceous borders to give a perennial quilt of colour before the summer flowers arrive. On wetter soils, they tend to disappear after the first year due to rot; so plant them in spring, then lift after flowering, store and replant in autumn.

PLANT BULBS IN EARLY WINTER

1 If you plan to leave bulbs in the border, plant 15–20cm (6–8in) deep so they're less likely to get accidentally weeded out or damaged when hoeing. If you plan to dig them up after flowering, plant only 10–15cm (4–6in) deep as they'll be easier to find. For a taste of the Dutch bulb fields, try growing in vivid rows or in blocks for cut flowers.

2 As flowering finishes, take away the petals to tidy them up. This helps to reduce the risk of rot, which is a particular problem with tulips grown in the same ground for years.

3 To lift bulbs, wait until leaves start dying down, then dig deeply to one side and lever them up, being careful not to break the leaves or scrape the bulbs. Lay bulbs flat in a box and place in a dry shed or greenhouse to dry. Then label up carefully and store until early winter in a dry shed, by which time the leaves will have withered away.

TIP
AVOID PESTS

To avoid pests and disease, don't plant tulips at the same time as daffodils in early autumn, wait until early winter. Any sooner and bulbs are prone to rotting and being nibbled by soil-dwelling eelworms. Damage shows up as weak, twisted leaves and bulbs often fail to flower. Always dig up and burn any weak malingering bulbs to prevent the spread of disease.

Tulips can look very sophisticated – It's not all lollipop reds and yellows – **black** is **back**.

OUR FAVOURITES

Darwin Hybrids – Larger and more rounded than the traditional spring-flowering tulip, these are the most popular tall tulip for bedding. Classed into singles and doubles, Darwin hybrids flower in late spring. The black-bloomed 'Queen of Night' (ABOVE) is the most fashionable.
H 70cm (28in)

Lily-flowered – Less stiff than Darwins, these elegant tulips flower in spring with slim-necks and pointed, out-curved petals. Pale pink 'Mariette' (ABOVE) has petals that flutter in the breeze. H 45–55cm (18–22in) 'Ballerina' (TOP) is a tropical-sunset range. H 45cm (18in)

Parrot – Similar to Darwins but the edges of each petal are fringed just like a feather. Flowering in late spring, 'Black Parrot' (ABOVE) is the most dramatic of tulips – definitely the fashionista's choice. H 50cm (20in)

Canna Lily

I love dynamic plants and you can't get more dynamic than canna lilies. Tropical through and through, their orchid-like flowers and speedy-growing leaves come in purples and stripes that can't help but get noticed. Grow them in containers or in a sunny-style exotic border with dahlias, rudbeckia and bananas. You can either pay more and buy ready-grown pot-plants in late spring or start off the roots or rhizomes in pots. For orange flowers, grow purple-leaved *Canna* 'Wyoming' or for stunning leaves, grow stripey 'Durban' or 'Striata'.

GROW FROM RHIZOMES

1 In early spring, buy rhizomes bagged up in the bulb section at the garden centre. They are not fully hardy, so don't plant straight out in the garden. Instead start rhizomes off in 20cm (8in) plastic pots of peat-free compost with the pointy bud facing upwards.

2 In late spring, or when frosts seem to have finished, plant out in a sunny sheltered spot, adding plenty of compost (or well-rotted manure if you can get it) to the soil. Plant 45cm (18in) apart. Then as it grows, feed with a balanced liquid fertilizer once a month during summer for really large leaves.

3 Canna lilies are traditionally dug up and stored in autumn, just after frosts have blackened the tops of the stems. With increasingly mild winters, this is becoming less necessary on well-drained soils and in warm city gardens. If you've only got one plant, it's safer to dig it up, if you've got a few, try leaving one in the ground to see if it survives the winter. The only disadvantage is they'll be slower to get started in spring than rhizomes started in the greenhouse.

TIPS

WEIGH DOWN CONTAINER CANNAS
To prevent plants being blown over in summer breezes, anchor containers to the ground by placing a few large pebbles in the base before planting.

HEIGHT 120–210cm (4–7ft) SPREAD 45cm (18in) CLIMATE ZONES 8–10

Canna 'Durban' has orange tiger stripes (RIGHT); for orange flowers grow purple-leaved 'Wyoming' (INSET)

4 Once rhizomes are dug up, cut down all the old foliage, then leave somewhere to dry off if the soil is wet.

5 Chop the clumps into manageable chunks and store for the winter by placing in buckets or wooden boxes lined with dry peat or multipurpose compost. Keep in a frost-free place, such as a porch or a greenhouse, until planting time in late spring.

If your **garden** looks boring after midsummer, plant some **dramatic canna lilies** for lush, **jungly leaves** and **tropical** flowers.

Get the Tropical Look

The tropical look is a fun style for a whole garden or even just for a small sunny corner. You don't need to grow greenhouse exotics, you can create the look with a mix of hardy evergreens, like palms and bamboo, along with vibrant hardy perennials, like crocosmia and day lilies. If you want to do a bit more work, add tender perennials like canna lilies and dahlias, and seed-sown annuals such as cosmos and rudbeckia for a richer effect. Because most tropical-style plants look good from midsummer onwards, you might want to add bulbs for spring and early summer interest too.

1 There are two essentials: good soil and shelter. So, first improve the soil by incorporating well-rotted manure or bags of soil improver from the garden centre. Dig in at least two buckets to every metre (3ft). For shelter, choose a warm sunny spot protected by the house to create a three-sided enclosure that will stop the worst of the winds, and capture the heat of the sun. Trellis or willow hurdle is ideal because the holes filter the wind, unlike solid fences, which can create extra turbulence.

2 The trick to planting is to neighbour plants with different foliage for a tapestry of colour, size and shape of leaf. Start with the largest plants first and spread evergreens like palms and bamboo through the borders for winter shape.

3 Hardy herbaceous plants in drifts between the larger plants can then be planted, leaving space for adding tender dahlia and canna for planting out after the frosts finish. Finally, plant summer-flowering bulbs like lilies, nerine and pineapple flower (*Eucomis*) in the gaps, marking the spot with a cane or a pebble.

Pink *Dahlia* 'Fascination', purple canna and yellow rudbeckia make for a tropical jungly look (TOP RIGHT)

4 Finally, a mulch of bark or pebbles will help to keep the weeds down and insulate the soil in winter. Using stone and gravel also captures the heat of the sun and speeds up growth.

TEN PLANTS FOR THE TROPICS

• *Dahlia* 'Fascination' – Bright pink flowers and dusky purple leaves from midsummer into autumn, page 108.

• **Bamboo** – Tall evergreen with an airy feel for instant height and colourful canes and leaves, page 28.

• **Banana** – Fun and fast-growing, with large, dramatic leaves, page 74.

• *Phormium tenax* – Structural evergreen with sword-shaped leaves in a variety of stripes and shades, page 35.

• *Cordyline australis* – Evergreen palm that slowly develops a trunk, page 34.

• *Clematis armandii* – Evergreen climber with scented white flowers in spring, page 77.

• *Canna* 'Wyoming' – Large leathery leaves in summer, page 68.

• *Euphorbia mellifera* – Evergreen lime-green leaves and scented flowers in late spring, page 38.

• *Eremurus* Ruiters Hybrids – Firework of flowers in canary yellows and orange, page 58.

• *Crocosmia* 'Lucifer' – Vibrant perennial with grassy leaves and red flowers in midsummer, page 106.

Hollyhock

Fig

Rose

Sweet Pea

Morning Glory

CHAPTER 4

Summer Climbers & Backdrops

Like church spires and chimney-tops, these climbers and backdrops give your garden a skyline – a break from the hum-drum of fences and house walls. They'll meet you eye-to-eye, giving you a summer garden above ground level blossoming with flowers, fruit and lush leaves. Classic summer blooms, roses and clematis will come back year after year, while annual climbers like 'Morning Glory' are sown afresh each spring. If you run out of room on walls and fences, wrap scented sweet peas around homemade steeples and give them centre-stage in a border.

And there's no need to restrict yourself to climbers – plants that need some sort of support – such as perennials like hollyhocks and delphiniums – will create a garden in the air supported on their stout, flower-smothered stems.

Clematis 'Viola' twines through *Rosa* 'Hiawatha' to cover a wall

Banana

Bananas (*Musa*), like palms and tree ferns, are fabulous plants. The Porsches of the horticultural world, they have giant leaves and racy growth – a single plant zooms from 30cm (1ft) to 1.8m (6ft) in just one season. The one to go for is the so-called hardy banana, *Musa basjoo*, available in garden centres in spring. Sadly, they're not hardy, so if you want to keep one through winter, it'll need wrapping up against the frost. But if you live in a city or have a frost-free garden, it will be fine.

KEEP BANANAS FROM YEAR TO YEAR

1 Plant out of the wind near a sunny wall where the reflected heat will make it grow like mad, adding plenty of compost or well-rotted (or garden centre-bought) manure to the hole. From late spring, water and feed with a dilute balanced liquid fertilizer for a constant supply of massive leaves until late summer.

2 Proud owners keep banana plants looking good by removing tatty lower leaves with secateurs – cut them right back to the trunk.

3 Keep an eye on weather forecasts and if temperatures consistently dip below freezing, it's time to say a tearful goodbye to this year's leaves and chop them off.

Get some hessian sacking, bubble-wrap or recycled carpet and loosely wrap it round the trunk, packing the insides with straw as you go.

START A PLANTATION

Bananas make babies! Look closely at the base of the stem and you'll see new plants – called 'offsets' – growing all round it. Chop each one off with a spade, levering some root too and grow on in large pots of multipurpose compost. Keep them frost-free through winter in a porch or greenhouse and plant out in spring.

HEIGHT & SPREAD 3x3m (10x10ft) after 3 years CLIMATE ZONES 7–10

With care, **banana** plants **survive** in a **cold** climate, so now no **tropical scheme** is complete **without** one.

4 Secure the hessian with twine to keep it snug all winter. If you do this, next year's display is guaranteed to be bigger and better! Take off the covers in early spring just as growth starts.

Bananas grow from shin-high to way above your head in just one season

Clematis

There are hundreds of types of clematis but generally speaking, they're either large with small flowers or small with big flowers! They're naturally wiry climbers evolved to clamber as high as they can before flowering and setting seed. That's fine in the wild, but in a garden you want a profusion of flowers lower down where they can be enjoyed. This is why books always go into great detail about pruning. You don't have to prune, you'll just get flowers high up and a leggy base. Just remember to prune after flowering or you risk losing next year's blooms.

HOW TO PLANT

1 Clematis are unusual in that you plant them 8cm (3in) deeper than they are in the pot, which encourages lots of stems to break from the base and more flowers. It also protects them from fungal diseases. The key to success is generous soil preparation so dig out a 30cm (12in) hole and dig in a forkful of well-rotted manure.

2 Before firming in, bury a plastic water bottle with its base cut off next to the root ball to help funnel water down to the roots. Then water well.

Though most clematis prefer to grow in sun, the roots like to stay cool, so cover around the base with broken paving stones, pebbles or a thick mulch of bark.

3 Always plant at the base of a suitable support, such as an obelisk, wall, trellis or fence, with wires and leave the canes in until the plant gets established. This is because the wiry stems are difficult to see and so easily stepped on and crushed.

PESTS

SNAILS, SLUGS AND APHIDS

Snails and slugs love clematis and are a major threat to their survival. Prevent snails by sprinkling organic pellets around the base of plants from early spring to midsummer and, to protect the delicate young shoots, use a nematode slug killer to eradicate soil-dwelling slugs. Look out for aphids (LEFT) in spring and spray with a contact insecticide if severe.

HEIGHT & SPREAD 2x10m (6x30ft) depending on variety CLIMATE ZONES 5–9

HOW TO PRUNE

Clematis are grouped by flowering time and are pruned accordingly. You can tell which group they fall into just by how they look and when they flower.

GROUP 1 The Earlies –
Medium to large climbers with small flowers including: *Clematis montana, C. armandii, C. macropetala, C. alpina.*
Pruning – either leave them alone or hack back with shears after flowering in late spring, but not in winter.

GROUP 2 The Middles –
Large flowers in early or mid-summer including large-flowered hybrids and *Clematis florida.*
Pruning – only trim after flowering if the plant is growing out of bounds. To rejuvenate an old plant, prune back to 30cm (12in) from the base in winter.

GROUP 3 The Lates –
Small to medium-sized flowers from midsummer to autumn including *Clematis viticella, C. jackmanii* and *C. texensis, C. tangutica, C. orientalis* and all named varieties.
Pruning – cut back to the lowest pair of healthy buds around 30cm (12in) from the base in late winter or early spring to prevent a bare base and all flowers at the top.

Clematis montana

Even the smallest of gardens has room for clematis. They'll flower profusely whether trained on walls, draped over pergolas or left to twine through borders.

Annual Climbers

The joy of annual climbers is that they are cheap to grow from packets of seeds and within no time will produce lots of leafy coverage and colourful flowers. They need a sheltered position in ordinary well-drained soil. Alternatively you can grow them in big 30cm (12in) or larger pots on a patio. They will die back as soon as the nights get cold and the frosts start but that needn't be a problem when it's so easy to raise fresh plants from seed again next year.

HOW TO SOW

1 Sow seed in spring in multipurpose compost, three seeds to a 12cm (5in) pot (except the slower *Rhodochiton*, which should be sown thinly in a tray and placed beneath a plastic bag on a warm windowsill). Pot on into individual pots as soon as they're up.

2 If climbing plants, like this Black-Eyed Susan, have to remain in pots for any length of time before being planted out they tend to become tangled up with each other. Put canes into the pot, tied together at the top, and keep them trained on to the supports.

3 Plant out where you want them to flower (when any frosts seem to have finished), at the base of a trellis, wigwam or to scramble over old garden tools. Place the plant on the shady side of its support so it grows through the frame towards the sun. Protect while small from slugs and snails.

BEST ANNUAL CLIMBERS

- **Purple Bell Vine** (*Rhodochiton atrosanguineum*) – Slow to germinate, but what it lacks at the start of the season it makes up for at the end. The hardiest of the selection, it flowers into winter in a frost-free place, the tubular flowers hanging beneath pink cocktail parasols which persist for weeks after the flowers have fallen. H 1m (3ft)

- **Black-Eyed Susan** (*Thunbergia alata*) – An easy classic with chocolate-centred tangerine flowers. Growth is spidery to start, gradually bushing up into dense clumps of arrow-shaped foliage. H 120cm (4ft)

- **Morning Glory** (*Ipomoea* 'Heavenly Blue') – Heart-shaped leaves and incredibly turquoise-blue flowers. It needs warmth and shelter – the leaves pale with cold – so don't sow until late spring, soaking seeds first to hasten germination. H 180–240cm (6–8ft)

- **Mexican Fiesta** (*Mina lobata*) – Vine-like leaves and flags of buds that burst into chilli-pepper red flowers that fade to orange and white. A pleasure to grow and the best of this collection for dense cover of trellis and garden divides. H 120–180cm (4–6ft)

Rhodochiton atrosanguineum (TOP)
***Ipomoea* 'Heavenly Blue'** (LEFT)
Mina lobata (BELOW LEFT)
Thunbergia alata (BELOW RIGHT)

Fig

Figs (*Ficus*) are exciting garden plants, easy and fast-growing. Although the books say you must restrict the roots for figs, they'll eventually fruit even without special planting and pruning. If fruit is your main aim, then train it on to a warm, sunny wall to ensure a long harvest period. But plants also do surprisingly well as free-standing shrubs even in semi-shaded city gardens. The crops of figs will be less profuse, but the leaves look just as large and glossy.

PLANT FOR FRUIT

1 Buy a container-grown plant in spring and choose a sunny spot at the base of a wall or fence. Dig a cube of soil 70cm (2–3ft) wide and deep. Line it with paving stones (or you could sink a large bin or barrel with the base sawn off). Put a layer of tightly packed broken bricks in the bottom and refill with soil, adding compost as you go. Then plant your fig in the middle.

2 If planted against a wall, figs can be fan-trained to provide more room in front and make stems more ornamental. Choose the sunniest wall you can find. As stems grow, tie them to wire, held proud of the wall by vine eyes that are screwed horizontally at 45cm (18in) intervals up the wall. Fan stems out 15cm (6in) apart and don't tie in too tightly to avoid strangling stems.

3 Side-shoots off the main branches bear fruit but can quickly outgrow the space. In spring, prune out every other side-shoot down to just one bud from the branch, concentrating on any frosted or fruited wood at the same time, and any that's in the way. Select those with the least baby figs on the branches (the embryo fruits that have over-wintered from last year and will swell ready for harvesting later in the summer). Once the fan is established (in about three years) always prune out some of the oldest wood too to stimulate young growth.

HEIGHT & SPREAD can be kept at 3x6m (9x18ft) fan-trained on a wall, up to 8m (24ft) as a tree

A wall-trained 'Brown Turkey' fig (ABOVE) **and ripe fruit** (RIGHT)

4 In summer, cut out the growing point of each new shoot to five leaves to encourage embryo fruits to form for next summer's crop.

TIPS

BUYING AND HARVESTING

The variety of fig you most commonly find is *F.* 'Brown Turkey' as it's the most reliably hardy, but for something more unusual, go to a specialist nursery. For best flavour, try early-fruiting pale-green *F.* 'White Marseilles', and for the most ornamental leaves, go for *F.* 'Brunswick'.

Figs are ripe when a dewdrop of sugary sap appears at the base of the fruit or the outside of the skin just starts to split. Pick immediately and eat with soft cheeses, or spread straight on to toast like marmalade.

Ficus 'Brunswick' has the most **beautiful** leaves, definitely the one that **Adam** and **Eve** would choose for a night out!

Can be kept smaller with pruning CLIMATE ZONE 7

Roses

For a robust and easy plant, buy a shrub rose. Many have a romantic old-fashioned look and are ideal for a border, either trained on obelisks as small climbers or as free-standing shrubs. Though they look very natural, many are modern-bred varieties with in-built disease-resistance and make wonderful cut flowers. They're tough plants and they thrive in heavy clays, where it's a battle to grow anything else. There are also many good climbers and large ramblers which are ideal for growing up fences or to enhance a bare wall.

PLANTING A SHRUB ROSE

1 You can buy a rose in one of two ways, as a containerized plant throughout the year, or more cheaply as a bare-root plant by mail order from a specialist nursery in winter, where you'll get a much better selection. As soon as they arrive, remove from packaging and either plant immediately or cover roots in a bag of compost until planting.

2 Prune back stems to 10cm (4in) just above an outward-facing bud, and trim any straggly or broken roots at the same time.

3 Choose a day when the ground isn't frozen to plant. Soak roots for an hour or two before planting, then dig a hole twice as large as the spread of the roots. Dig a forkful of well-rotted manure or compost into the base. Place the plant in the hole with the scion (the point where all the stems emerge from the roots) 5cm (2in) below soil level.

4 Backfill with soil, avoiding any air pockets between the soil and roots and firming gently as you go. Finally, pour on a can of water to settle the roots and mulch with more manure or compost.

PESTS

FUNGAL DISEASES

Roses growing poorly, and weak, disease-prone varieties are more likely to be attacked by fungal diseases. Control with a proprietary rose fungicide.
RUST (TOP) – Orange pustules on under-sides of leaves. In minor attacks just pick off. Otherwise spray.
POWDERY MILDEW (LEFT) – Tends to happen when roses are dry at the base and in muggy summers. The best prevention is watering well and mulching before high summer.
BLACKSPOT (BOTTOM) – Pick off leaves at the first sign and spray stems and leaves with a fungicide as damage limitation.

TIPS FOR HEALTHY ROSES

- Deadhead – To keep flowers coming, take off the dead flowers as soon as they're over, trimming back 5cm (2in) below the blooms.

- Feed – As young leaves emerge in spring, spray plants once a month with a dilute seaweed feed. This helps thicken the foliage and is an organic alternative to chemical fungicides for reducing the risk of fungal diseases.

- Watch out for aphids – Spraying with seaweed will also reduce the risk of aphids on the juicy tips. Alternatively spray with a natural insecticide containing pyrethrum.

BEST SHRUB ROSES, CLIMBERS AND RAMBLERS

- *Rosa* 'Buff Beauty' – A good choice for poor soils this summer-long flowering, lightly fragrant hybrid musk suits an obelisk or as a climber for a small fence.
H&S 150x120cm (5x4ft)

- *R.* 'Blush Noisette' – One of the longest-flowering roses with lightly scented clusters of candyfloss-pink flowers. Grow this as a shrub or small climber.
H&S 220x120cm (7x4ft)

- *R.* 'Cornelia' – Good all-rounder with bronzy foliage and fragrant, continuous apricot-pink hybrid musk flowers summer-long to autumn.
H&S 150x150cm (5x5ft)

- *R.* 'Macmillan Nurse' – Modern shrub rose with old-fashioned rosettes, glossy, dark-green very healthy foliage.
H&S 1x1m (3x3ft)

- *R. rugosa* – Shell-pink flowers and yellow autumn leaves, good hedging plant and for rough soils.
H&S 180x150cm (6x5ft)

- *R.* 'New Dawn' – A climber for light shade (repeats in sun) with pale pink neat flowers.
H&S 3x2.4m (10x8ft)

- *R.* 'Rambling Rector' – A good rambler for a large tree or on top of a shed with fragrant clusters of tiny poached-egg flowers in summer.
H&S 9x3.5m (25x15ft)

- *R.* 'Sophie's Perpetual' – An old repeat-flowering China rose with silvery-pink scented flowers cupped in petals of a deeper purple-pink.
H&S 250x120cm (8x4ft)

- *R.* 'Madame Alfred Carriere' – Classic climber with creamy-pink double scented flowers, good for light shade.
H&S 3.5x3m (12x10ft)

Rosa 'Cornelia'

Rosa 'Macmillan Nurse'

Rosa rugosa

Rosa 'Sophie's Perpetual'

Sweet Pea

Sweet peas (*Lathyrus*) are fast-growing cottage-garden climbers. They are sown from seed every year and live just until the frosts. They're easy to raise from seed (you can buy ready-sown seedlings from garden centres in spring too) and just a few plants are enough to make scented summer cover for a 180cm (6ft) trellis or wicker wigwam. They thrive on sun, rich soils and plenty of watering, and are even better in rainy summers. There are lots of different varieties, some with bigger flowers, some very frilly, but for delicious perfume go for the old dainty varieties, like *Lathyrus* 'Cupani' or 'Painted Lady'.

START FROM SEED

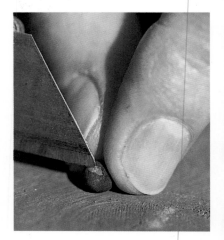

1 Sow seeds five to a 10cm (4in) pot of seed-sowing compost in autumn or spring. Autumn-sown plants flower about a fortnight earlier, but need keeping in a cold-frame or greenhouse until the frosts are over. Some seed packets recommend 'chitting' the seeds – this means chipping off a tiny bit of the black outer coat of the seed in order to help germination but if you're sowing at the ideal time, it doesn't seem to be needed.

2 When seedlings appear, split pots into clumps of twos and threes and pot back into 10cm (4in) pots of multipurpose compost.

3 When seedlings get to about 20cm (8in) tall, nip off the top few centimetres of each shoot between finger and thumb to make them bushier, and so yield more flowers later.

TIP

WARD OFF MICE

If you live in the countryside, mice and voles are likely to sniff out pea seeds (they love most large seeds) and devour them before they come up. Put them off the scent by dipping seeds in a little paraffin before sowing. It doesn't hurt the seeds and the mice are none the wiser!

Sweet peas have a heavenly, creamy scent, all **innocence** and **nostalgia** wrapped into one – irresistible decoration for the house.

4 Plant out in the garden from the end of spring onwards in a sunny spot where they can scramble over a support, such as an obelisk or trellis. If you get round to it in winter, add lots of manure to the soil and let it settle for a month or two for healthy, long-flowering plants. Otherwise, add lots of compost when planting and remember to water frequently.

5 Deadheading is essential for sweet peas to flower for any length of time or they stop and make seed. The best way is just to keep cutting lots of flowers for the house – they're so prolific there'll still be plenty of flowers in the garden.

Wigwam-trained *Lathyrus* **'Cupani'** (TOP AND BOTTOM RIGHT) **'Painted Lady'** (INSET LEFT)

Delphinium

Delphiniums have a quintessentially English garden look. Design-wise the colours of the bold hybrids are bright and unnatural, and the large flowers need propping up and protecting. That said, nothing beats them for back-of-the-border impact in early summer. If you want a more natural, airy look that fits better with grasses, go for the Belladonna group, which has the height without the stiffness and there is no need for staking.

HOW TO GROW

1 Buy plants in mid spring and plant in sun, in well-drained soil improved with well-rotted manure or compost, then water in well. If your soil is heavy, improve the drainage with horticultural grit and plant the crown on a mound 5cm (2in) higher than the surrounding soil to prevent rotting in winter.

2 Before leaves get above 30–45cm (12–18in) tall, stake using bamboo canes or plastic-coated stakes from the garden centre. A homemade grid made from willow looks most natural – see how to make this on page 36.

3 Once the first flush of flowers has finished, cut the whole flower-spike down to the ground to encourage a second flush. Feed with a balanced liquid fertilizer to give the plant a boost and make it flower again. In winter cut the spent stems down to the ground.

HEIGHT & SPREAD 150–200cm (5–6ft) x 57cm (30in) CLIMATE ZONE 3

Just like old-fashioned ladies **teetering** on their canes, **delphiniums** have aristocratic poise, standing **aloof** over the hoi polloi of early **summer** plants.

WATCH OUT FOR SLUGS

Young delphiniums are most vulnerable to attack by slugs and snails, so water in with a dilute solution of the biological control containing nematodes, or use organic slug pellets. But slugs aren't only a problem when plants are growing, their herbaceous crowns are vulnerable to slugs when they have died down in winter. This often explains why delphiniums are either weak or don't make a come-back in subsequent springs. Sprinkle a proprietary organic slug barrier or sharp sand over the crown when it dies down in autumn and keep it topped up through winter. To keep on top of slugs in spring, water the crown and surrounding soil again with a nematode drench poured on to plants before growth starts.

Hollyhock

Hollyhocks (*Alcea*) are sultry high-summer plants, great for the back of the border or for a cottage garden look, propped along the edge of a brick path. Their lofty flowers will clothe trellis fast while waiting for climbers to grow. Though a hardy perennial, their susceptibility to the fungal disease rust on the foliage, means they're often short-lived, but regenerate naturally from self-sown seedlings. There are two types – *Alcea rosea*, which comes in pastel rose pinks, apricots, lemons and white, double and single flowered; and also the more refined fig-leaved *Alcea rosea* 'Nigra' – adored for its shiny, black-purple cups.

SOW OR PLANT

1 Buy in spring and plant out in full sun in any ordinary garden soil and water in well. Alternatively, they're easy to sow from seed in spring or summer in pots to plant out in autumn. Spraying with a dilute solution of seaweed tonic can help strengthen the leaf cuticles and ward off future fungal problems.

2 Rust patrols are necessary from early on to keep plants in tip-top condition, as young plants can be killed by the disease. They're more likely to get rust when they're too dry, so keep well watered. The rust shows up as orange spots on the undersides of leaves and then a brown mottling on the surface. It's very common but doesn't spread to other plants except weedy mallows and occasionally *Lavatera*, but it will spread between hollyhocks. Pick off affected leaves and burn them. Cutting down the whole plant and burning the stems, along with collected leaves in winter should control its spread.

3 Keep plants looking their best by removing any tatty leaves and, once the flowers finish, either leave flower-spikes to seed or cut down before the seed falls.

TIP

KNOW YOUR
SEEDLING

Hollyhocks are self-sowers, so once your plant has flowered in the garden, it's likely to come up of its own accord in sunny spots. Make sure you don't accidentally weed it out by knowing what the seedling looks like.

Alcea filicifolia (RIGHT)
A. 'Nigra' (BELOW RIGHT)

Hollyhocks are archetypal chocolate-box flowers. Even without the **picket fences** and thatched eaves, they say 'cottage garden'.

Classic Rose Training

Roses are a gardener's favourite plant and lend themselves to artful weaving and training to look even more magical. Training is also practical as, left to their own devices, many shrub roses will grow as wide as they are tall. Spiralling them around supports brings up their flowerheads to a height where their fragrance can be enjoyed while freeing up space at their feet for other flowers.

TRAIN SHRUB AND CLIMBING ROSES

When trained against a wall or fence, shrub roses should be pruned like climbers rather than shrub roses. A well-trained climber is healthier, and will produce more flowers with blooms even on low stems. The winter stems will be an ornamental feature in their own right.

Rosa 'New Dawn' after training in winter (FAR RIGHT) and in full flower in early summer (BELOW)

1 To provide support use plastic-coated or galvanized wires fixed at 45cm (18in) intervals on to vine eyes. Run these up the wall horizontally to give the best flexibility for tying in stems. New plants need to grow for a year before they are ready for this.

2 The idea is to train stems as close to horizontal as possible as this encourages them to flower well. First, prune any side-shoots from the main stems down to two buds as this makes them easier to handle and promotes flowers along the branches. Cut out any old or damaged wood while you're there. Then, tie on the stems, arching each over the face of the brickwork spacing them 10cm (4in) apart.

How you train the climber depends on what space it's going to fill – if you have a large bare wall, a perfect fan shape is best. If you want it to frame a window, train the main stem to curve up and around it with no growth beneath it.

TRAINING INTO A SPIRE

Spires are another option for training roses, using five hazel rods bound at the top with twine. Copper pipe or painted bamboo make a good substitute too. Spires are ideal for roses situated deep in a border as they add instant height. Position the struts of the spire next to the rose, then wind the briars on to the structure, securing the stems in place with twine as you go.

This wigwam method is ideal for roses that grow between 1.2–3m (4–10ft), such as the stripey hybrid perpetual 'Ferdinand Pichard', which grows to 1.5x1.2m (5x4ft) and has plentiful repeat flowers.

Rosa 'Ferdinand Pichard'
flowering in early
summer (ABOVE)

TIP

BUYING HAZEL

Hazel rods are usually sold by thatchers and local woodland trusts, so check out telephone listings for numbers. They don't charge a lot of money and what they do charge goes back into regenerating ancient woodland.

Training a rose's bare stems transforms it into a living garden sculpture.

Aquilegia

Peony

Cosmos

CHAPTER 5

Flowers to fill Spaces

Flowers come in all shapes, shades and sizes. This chapter is devoted to flowers – sowing, growing, cutting them, and aiming to have more than you know what to do with! As a rule, flowering plants are categorized by how long they live: those that last for one summer are called 'annuals'; those that flower in their second year from sowing are 'biennials'; while those that hide away for winter beneath the soil and spring up year after year are called 'perennials'. Ideally, every garden should have a mixture of each group to ensure you have colour through all the seasons.

Traditionally, the annuals go in containers and need to be replaced but they also make fast-growing fillers between permanent plants, while perennials tend to live out their lives in the border amongst surrounding trees and shrubs.

Dahlia

Rudbeckia

Crocosmia 'Lucifer' with Ferrari-red flowers goes at full throttle in midsummer

Hellebore

In the deep cold of early spring when little else is stirring, the hellebore (*Helleborus*) produces its striking cup-shaped flowers.

If you haven't grown them before, the best to try is the Lenten rose, *Helleborus orientale*, with its flowers in freckled purples, whites and pinks which make a change from all those early yellows. If you catch the collector's bug, you'll want to splash out on expensive dark purples and named varieties. Keep them well away from less showy types, to be sure the seedling offspring are as special as the parents, rather than motley hybrids.

PLANT IN SUN OR LIGHT SHADE

1 Choose a spot that's sheltered from harsh winds, say under a tree or in the lee of a hedge, because although the plants are hardy, wintry winds and rain can mark the delicate petals. Before you plant, fork in garden compost or leafmould to make it rich and moisture-retentive, about half a bucketful to every square foot 30x30cm (12x12in). Arrange three plants to every 1m (4ft) for best impact and water them in.

2 Mulch between them with 2.5cm (1in) of soil improver or more compost. This cover improves the appearance of the soil and accentuates the petals, but primarily acts as a nursery bed for the seed that drops from the flowers.

3 In late autumn, prepare the way for the flowers by cutting back tatty leaves to the base leaving the fresh central leaves to develop along with the flowers. Mulch again to enhance the look.

4 In summer, look out for seedlings around the plant. If you don't want more, weed them out or carefully dig up with a trowel and transplant to other suitable parts of the garden.

HEIGHT & SPREAD 45x60cm (18x24in) CLIMATE ZONE 6

Even when the weather's freezing cold and **wintry**, hellebores make it **worth** going out for a closer **look**.

Helleborus 'Ashwood's Variety' (RIGHT). It's always worth turning up the pendulous flowers for a closer look

PESTS

LOOK OUT FOR LEAF BLOTCH

Leaf blotch is a fungal disease that shows up as black patches or circles on both sides of the leaves, and may wither the stem. All hellebore species are affected but Lenten roses can have the disease without it seeing off the plant. But if spots get bigger than 2.5cm (1in) across, cut off the affected leaves and burn. If it happens a lot, it may be because your hellebores are growing in a soil that is too wet, so try digging them up and moving to a drier part of the garden.

Aquilegia

If you plant aquilegia one year, you'll have them popping up all over the place from self-sown seed the next! They're invaluable for colouring early summer, in the gap between the last of the tulips and the beginning of the roses. For a cottage garden look, plump for the traditional Granny's Bonnet (*Aquilegia vulgaris*), blue, pink, white and every shade between. If you want something a bit more special for a herbaceous border, lovely 'Nora Barlow' has unusual spiky pink flowers with pale-green tips. For a bolder take on the flower, try one of the North American McKana Hybrids.

PLANT OR SOW

1 Choose a lightly shaded spot and plant in spring or autumn in groups of three or five, spaced 45cm (18in) apart for a natural look.

2 After flowering, you've got two choices – either let plants go to seed and self-sow, or pick seed capsules and sow seed where you want it. (Self-sown plants aren't usually the same colour as the parent, so if you're sticking to a colour scheme, chop off and bin the seedheads before they scatter.)

3 If you do want self-sown plants, be careful not to accidentally weed them out when hoeing so get to know how the seedlings look.

WHAT TO DO IF LEAVES TURN WHITE …

Aquilegia leaves often succumb to powdery mildew after flowering in midsummer and this makes the leaves look white and tatty. Cut off all the foliage down to the ground and they'll bounce back with fresh new leaves, like spring all over again!

HEIGHT & SPREAD 60x45cm (2x1ft) CLIMATE ZONES 3–8

Aquilegia are an essential cottage garden plant and make long-lasting cut flowers for the house, too.

Aquilegia (ABOVE) are great for bringing life to shade in dark purples or the pale double heritage variety A. 'Powder Blue' (LEFT), or try the lovely A. 'Nora Barlow' (INSET ABOVE LEFT)

Herbaceous Peony

There's a lot to like about peonies (*Paeonia*). They start looking good from the moment their red shoots emerge in spring until their large and glossy leaves tint and go to ground in winter. Most spectacular of all are their flowers – as large as saucers and often scented – they open in early summer, depending on the variety, from globe-like buds. They're very long lived, so if you take on an overgrown garden, there's invariably a peony still thriving, despite overcrowding and years in the wilderness!

HOW TO PLANT

1 Plant in sun or light shade in well-composted soil as containerized plants any time, or buy as bare-root plants in autumn. Plant containerized peonies so that the top of the pot compost is at the same level as the surrounding soil; plant bare-root peonies with buds 1cm (½in) below soil level.

2 In early spring, once the buds emerge, mulch around them with garden compost and stake with pea sticks or plastic hoops so that the leaves grow up and hide any supporting structure.

3 In autumn, in poorer soils, feed with a light dressing of slow-release fertilizer such as bonemeal.

Paeonia 'Rosea Plena' **blooming with the wallflowers in late spring** (FAR RIGHT)

TRANSPLANTING PEONIES

Peonies don't need lifting and dividing like other herbaceous plants and received wisdom says they don't like being moved. However, if your plant isn't flowering, it could be overcrowded and hungry or buried too deeply. In mid-autumn, dig it up with a spade, chopping large clumps over 30cm (1ft) wide in half and re-plant into well-composted soil. Plant so that the crown is just below the soil level. Don't panic if young plants don't flower in the first year – some varieties, especially the more unusual ones, often need a couple of summers to get to flowering size.

HEIGHT & SPREAD 70x45cm (30x18in) CLIMATE ZONE 6

EASY PEONIES

● *Paeonia officinalis* 'Rubra Plena'
– The classic old cottage garden
double red variety with wonderful
flouncy, scented flowers.

● *P. lactiflora* 'Bowl of Beauty' –
A luxuriant pink cup containing
a frilly 'cut' lemon centre.

● *P. o.* 'Rosea Plena' (in bud) –
Silver-pink double flowers fading
to pale peach.

Peonies are like film stars – they always look good, they're seriously sexy and never show their age!

Poppy

Poppies (*Papaver*) have tissue-paper petals and a whimsical look. There are perennial, biennial and annual types and all make colourful fillers, given sun and well-drained soil. Which one is right for you depends on how much space you have, and whether you want to buy a ready-grown plant or to sow poppies from seed.

SELECTING THE RIGHT POPPY

ORIENTAL POPPY (*Papaver orientale*) – The straight species is pillar-box red, but if you want softer colours to combine in a border, try the salmon-pink *P. o.* 'Charming' or the mauve *P. o.* 'Patty's Plum'.
H&S 90cm (36in)

TO GROW – Plant in sun in any good garden soil, stake in spring and once the flowers finish and the plant flops, tidy up by cutting off the old flower-spikes and the oldest leaves right down to the crown of emerging fresh leaves at the base. A very reliable garden plant that design-wise looks best in clumps dotted among other plants.

(CLOCKWISE FROM TOP LEFT)
Papaver orientale 'Elam pink'
P. orientale, furry in bud
P. o. 'Charming' is salmon-pink

CLIMATE ZONES *P. somniferum* 7; *P. orientale* 3; *P. nudicaule* 2

OPIUM POPPY (*Papaver somniferum*) – The sun-ripened sap of this plant is the raw ingredient of opium in arid regions but here where summers are relatively cool and short it makes a colourful but harmless annual filler plant. The tall, slim, blue-grey leaves are topped with single flowers (or double in the case of *P. somniferum paeoniflorum*) in pinks, mauves and dusky purples that teeter above their stems like the giant hats of ladies at Ascot races. Opium poppies are great colonizers for sunny gravel gardens and are so easy they'll take over if left to their own devices. H&S 100x80cm (40x8in)

TO GROW – The trick to control their spread is to pull up the plants as flowers finish, sparing only a few of the best. Pick seedheads as soon as they rattle (seeds look black) and sprinkle – not too liberally – where you want them to flower next year.

Papaver somniferum in flower (ABOVE) **and its pepper-pot seedheads** (RIGHT)

ICELAND POPPY (*Papaver nudicaule*) is classed as a biennial (or short-lived perennial if you're lucky) and is a cottage garden classic with olive-green foliage, wiry stems and flowers in dilute cordial colours from lemon barley to orange squash. It has the delicate look of wild poppies but with more impact, so Iceland poppies are the choice where space is limited. H&S 60cm (24in)

TO GROW – Sow seed as for opium poppies, scattering thinly in an open spot where you want the flowers – by staggering sowing between spring and early summer, you can achieve a succession of flower. *P. o.* 'Meadow Pastels' is a reliable and commonly available variety or buy as ready-grown plants in spring.

Papaver nudicaule (LEFT)
Double-pink Papaver somniferum (ABOVE)

Cosmos

Cosmos aren't hardy, but make covetable garden plants. Annual cosmos (*Cosmos bipinnatus*) is sown from seed in spring and planted out after the frosts. Then the work's done – sit back and enjoy feathery plumes of foliage and flowers until the autumn, in shades of shell-pink, magenta and white. Chocolate cosmos (*Cosmos atrosanguineus*) is a tuberous perennial loved for its chocolate-coloured flowers and matching scent. It is easiest if grown in pots so you can simply move it indoors for protection through winter.

GROW ANNUAL COSMOS

1 Sow seed in spring in a greenhouse, following the guide on page 24. It's an easy seed to sow as seedlings appear in just a couple of days.

2 Prick out into individual 9cm (3in) pots when seedlings are large enough to handle and grow on in a frost-free greenhouse until late spring, when you can plant out in the garden depending on when the last frost is in your area.

3 Before planting, pinch out the tips to make them bushy.

4 Plant out in ordinary garden soil. Don't worry about improving the soil as this only tends to promote lots of leaves instead of flowers. Space 45cm (18in) apart and water in well.

5 As soon as they come into flower, keep picking for the house and deadhead regularly to keep blooms coming.

Cosmos 'Versailles Tetra'

HEIGHT & SPREAD 45x30cm (18x12in) CLIMATE ZONES *C. bipinnatus* 3–9; *C. atrosanguineus* 8–10

GROW CHOCOLATE COSMOS

1 Buy in flower in midsummer or more cheaply as tubers from the bulb section of the garden centre in spring. Plant tubers straight into a pot of peat-free multipurpose compost. During the growing season deadhead, water regularly and feed with a balanced liquid fertilizer once a month.

2 After the last frost, place on the cool side of your patio and water lots as foliage wilts in hot conditions. Remember to watch out for slugs.

3 As soon as stems start to die down in autumn, it's time to bring the pots under cover in a frost-free greenhouse or shed where they can stay dry and last through winter.

4 In mid spring water the pots and young growth will appear. This is the time to divide tubers for extra plants. Knock the plant out of the pot and tease tuberous roots into handful-sized clumps. Then re-pot into fresh compost for summer.

Grow annual cosmos for **armfuls** of cut flowers or chocolate cosmos for **wafts** of sweet-smelling **chocolate** on your patio.

Cosmos atrosanguineus

Day Lily

The day lily (*Hemerocallis*) gets its name because each flower only lasts a day, but come by the hundred throughout summer. Not to be confused with real lilies which are bulbs (*see* page 64), day lilies do make a good substitute, particularly where soils are poor. Some are softly scented, particularly the yellows, and they have a strong profile that contrasts well with more wispy flowers of high summer. Day lilies come in a wide range of colours through cream, yellow, orange, red and purple. They're tough and fairly trouble-free in terms of pests and diseases.

HOW TO GROW DAY LILIES

1 Plant in moist but well-drained soil in sun or light shade. Darker-red varieties such as *Hemerocallis* 'Stafford' or *H.* 'Starling' prefer dappled shade or they tend to scorch and lose their colour. Their grassy leaves make them suitable for planting in drifts, and they contrast well with many other plants.

2 Pinch off old, shrivelled flowers so they don't distract from the new ones, and when there are finally no more flowerbuds to come, cut off the whole flower-spike at the base.

3 In winter when foliage dies back, cut it off at ground level. This allows the spring foliage to come up cleanly and removes a hiding place for slugs and snails through winter.

HEIGHT & SPREAD 50–80cm (20–30in) x 40cm (16in) CLIMATE ZONE 4

Day lilies are the flower made for people without green fingers.

TIPS

EAT YOUR FLOWERS

Day lilies are edible, with a crunchy texture and sweet, faintly oniony flavour. Use them to add a splash of colour to summer meals. Use the petals in salads, the buds in stir-fries or stuff the entire flower with a soft cheese.

The best-tasting blooms are the yellow and orange varieties as some of the reds are bitter. Remove the anthers and stamens from the centre before eating and if you can't tell the difference between a day lily and a lily, don't eat! Lilies are poisonous.

Day lilies look like lilies but are much tougher; *Hemerocallis* 'Stafford' (ABOVE), *H.* 'Golden Chimes' (INSET RIGHT)

Crocosmia

Crocosmia are fantastic perennials for adding fiery colour to borders from mid to late summer. The larger the flower, the less hardy they are, but most common types available in garden centres are hardy and grow in sun or light shade. They absolutely thrive in well-drained soils in moist coastal climates. The sword-shaped leaves are attractive too, having a lush, grassy look, and some varieties, such as yellow-flowered *Crocosmia* 'Solfatare' and *C.* 'Dusky Maiden', have bronzy foliage. Although available as dry corms (like bulbs), they establish more quickly from pot-grown plants.

HOW TO GROW

1 For a reliably hardy variety go for scarlet *Crocosmia* 'Lucifer' or 'Emberglow' and plant as pot-grown plants in autumn or spring, in soil improved with garden compost. In heavy soils, it's essential to add grit to the planting hole to improve drainage.

2 Water-in well and keep well watered with a sprinkler hose in drier districts. Regularly spray water over the leaves to deter red spider mite. This shows up as yellowing, speckled leaves and severely weakens plants.

3 Only lift and divide plants if they become congested and flowering is reduced. Do it ideally in early spring or autumn if you have to, splitting plants into saucer-sized clumps before replanting.

HEIGHT & SPREAD 60–120cm (2–4ft) x 30cm (1ft) CLIMATE ZONES 5–6

4 All types – hardy and tender – benefit from mulching over the crown with bark or straw in autumn.

TIP

PLANTING TENDER CROCOSMIA

Wait until spring to plant tender varieties like *Crocosmia* 'Solfatare' and *C.* 'Star of the East'. Position 5cm (2in) deeper in the soil than planted in the pot for better winter protection.

Crocosmia are tough and very pest resistant, even rabbits don't like them! *C.* 'Emily McKenzie' (RIGHT)

Dahlia

Like most exotics dahlias make an explosion of colour right through to the frosts in autumn. Fantastic space fillers, growing from nothing to around 1m (4ft) in just a few months, dahlias come in flamingo-pinks, like 'Fascination', and tango-orange, such as 'Vulcan', perfect for exotic schemes, as well as softer shades for traditional borders. They are available as pot-grown plants in garden centres, but if you don't mind a bit of extra work, the widest choice are sold as tubers (bulb-like, swollen roots) in early spring by mail order specialists.

GIVE TUBERS THE RIGHT START

1 In early spring, plant tubers into 30cm (12in) pots of moist multipurpose compost with the join uppermost. Keep indoors or in a greenhouse where they won't be frosted and start watering once green shoots appear.

2 In late spring, plant out in a sunny spot in the garden, allowing 90cm (3ft) between plants, mixing with sunflowers and canna lilies for an exotic look or to carry on from peonies and roses. If your garden is quite windy, it's a good idea to stake with bamboo canes.

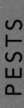

PESTS

WHAT TO WATCH OUT FOR
Earwigs, those 2cm (¾in) thin creatures with pseudo-pincers on the back, are fairly harmless insects, but they do chew petals, and their favourites are chrysanthemums, clematis and dahlias.

They don't like it hot, and so hole up somewhere dark and comfy during the day, meaning they can be caught in traps made from upturned pots stuffed with straw or an old tea towel and placed near flowers on bamboo canes. Discard as your conscience dictates!

Dahlia **'David Howard'**
(TOP RIGHT) **and**
D. **'Vulcan'** (RIGHT) **both blossom luxuriously throughout the summer**

HEIGHT & SPREAD 90–120cm (3x5ft) x 60–90cm (2–3ft) CLIMATE ZONES 8–10

Dahlias have made a **comeback** after years in the fashion **wilderness** thanks to the trend for **bold** colours.

TIP

DEADHEAD AND LIFT
Once plants start to flower, deadheading will ensure the show continues but don't mix up flowerbuds, like tight buttons, with spent blooms which are more elongated and teardrop-shaped. Keep picking lots of flowers for the house because that's what makes them just keep coming all summer!

At the end of the season, once frost blackens foliage, lift tubers as for cannas (*see page 69*).

Red Hot Poker

Great for spikes of summer colour, red hot pokers (*Kniphofia*) are easy to grow and have grassy evergreen (or semi-evergreen) leaves. Old favourites like *Kniphofia* 'Royal Standard' and *K. caulescens* make large clumps with glowing red and orange cobs that soar towards the sky. The late-summer flowering red hot pokers are star candidates for tropical-style plantings, looking fiery and exotic alongside canna lilies, crocosmia and dahlias. Recent introductions are smaller and more subtle with caramel flowers, such as *K.* 'Toffee Nosed'.

PLANT IN WELL-DRAINED SOIL

1 Plant in spring in sun and well-drained soil but not too dry in summer. Because red hot pokers can rot in clay soils, add grit and organic matter to the planting hole if your soil is heavy and prone to be wet in winter.

2 Once clumps start to become too large, lift and divide (as described for Michaelmas daisies on page 118) in spring, then replant in drifts.

3 Protect the roots from severe winter cold by mulching around the plant with bark in autumn.

GOOD FOR URBAN GARDENS

Red hot poker's evergreen leaves and architectural flowers look fantastic against brickwork, buildings and garden features. Use them as stand-alone plants on the corner of a path or as sentinels either side of a seat in the sun. Not all red hot pokers are red and orange, some are buttercup coloured, such as *K.* 'Sunningdale Yellow', or caramel, like *K.* 'Shining Sceptre'.

HEIGHT & SPREAD 60x150cm (2x5ft) CLIMATE ZONES 5–10

Kniphofia caulescens is robust and stocky, forming large clumps; *K. 'Sunningdale Yellow'* (INSET TOP) and *K. 'Shining Sceptre'* (INSET BOTTOM) are better for small borders

4 Give the leaves a tidy up in autumn and again in mid spring, by gently tugging out old, dead leaves from around the base. Cut the last flowers for the house before the frost takes them.

Once the stalwarts of the 1970s, red hot pokers have been reinvented for the Noughties with more compact shapes and subtler shades.

Rudbeckia

Summer is a game of two halves, with roses and foxgloves blooming in the first and a whole new team colouring the second. Rudbeckia comes into play after half-time, saving your borders from looking drab as summer turns to autumn, and flowering well through the rain. They are classic yellow daisies with a twist, having a black cone in the centre of each (hence its other name of cone flower), which is velvety as a puppy's nose.

ANNUALS OR PERENNIALS

There are two types – annuals that are sown from seed in pots every spring and last just one year and perennials that live year after year. All you need to grow either type is a sunny or lightly shaded spot and to water young plants if it's dry. If you fancy having a go with planting seeds, *see* the Gardening Techniques section on page 24. Sow in a greenhouse and plant out after the frosts – they are slow starters, so wait until roots are showing at the base before potting on.

The annuals are more interesting and flowery, for example, the shaggy yellow pom-poms of *Rudbeckia* 'Double Delight', (ABOVE).

The best rudbeckia perennials include *R.* 'Goldsturm' (ABOVE) which is thigh-high and looks great behind sedum and grasses, and the much larger *R.* 'Herbstsonne' (H 180cm/6ft), which does a good job at the back of the border, hiding fences and filling big gaps. The stems can be cut off at ground level from autumn or left until early spring to provide some interesting winter structure in the garden.

R. 'Cherokee Sunset' (LEFT)

HEIGHT & SPREAD Annuals 75–90cm (30–36in) x 40cm (16in); Perennials 60x45cm (24x18in) CLIMATE ZONES 3–10

DEADHEAD ANNUALS

You don't need to deadhead perennial rudbeckia, but annuals stop flowering unless you cut the spent flower-stems right back to the first leaf.

Cutting flowers for the house will have the same effect. Rudbeckia lasts for over a week, if you do it the way flower arrangers do. Take stems of flowers that are just opening in the morning, if possible, strip off all the leaves and place the stems straight into buckets of water.

Annual rudbeckia are great peek-a-boo plants for rustic driftwood and picket fences

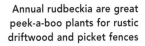

Rudbeckia shines on through the worst that autumn throws at it, continuing to flower despite rain, wind and even the first frosts.

Salvia

You'll love herbaceous salvia. Even in the first year, they fill gaps fast with violet-blue spikes making a vivid purple haze in summer right through into autumn. While many fashionable salvia are on the tender side, *Salvia* x *superba* and *S. nemorosa* are very hardy and look great in any border in sun. In winter they go to ground like other herbaceous plants, then bounce back into growth in spring and set seed too, giving you new plants for free.

FILL A SPACE FAST

1 Plant salvia in sun, in well-drained borders. If you have a lot of space to fill fast, plant them in groups of three or five, and they'll soon cover the bare ground. They're good under roses to sprawl and help hide the rose's leggy stems.

2 In high summer, as the top spikes of flowers fade, the bracts left behind still give colour, but deadheading these encourages the new spikes beneath to break into flower, giving two or more further flushes. Leave the last of the flowers to 'go over' in late summer as the outer cases make for colourful autumn and winter shapes.

3 Clear dead stems in late winter to make way for the fresh spring growth. In spring, look out for seedlings. Dig them up carefully with plenty of soil around the roots and transplant to where you want them to flower. Remember to water them in well.

HEIGHT& SPREAD 60x45cm (24x18in) CLIMATE ZONES 5–8

Salvia nemerosa

forms clumps and makes a **great addition** to any **border** with their **dramatic** purple spikes.

TIP

CUT FOR THE HOUSE

Salvias make long-lasting cut flowers for the house, providing a frothy frame, and an alternative to a foliage backdrop for larger blooms like dahlias and roses.

Pick in the morning and plunge straight into water to prevent the stems from curling.

Salvia nemorosa **'Ostfriesland' is the hardiest salvia you can get** (LEFT)

Penstemon

Penstemons are jingly, airy perennials, like foxgloves only smaller and more colourful. They flower from midsummer and can be one of the last things blooming in autumn. They're easy too – just keep an eye on border-grown plants from year to year, as they go into a decline if other plants crowd them. Often described as slightly tender, it's winter wet not cold that carries them off, so improving drainage on heavy soil is the key. Alternatively, take cuttings in late summer – these will be just the right size for planting out and flowering the following summer.

HOW TO GROW

1 Buying penstemons in flower is one of life's great pleasures. Real collectors' plants, they have charming names and flowers, and planting them out gives an instant lift to the garden. Plant in full sun and add half a bucket of grit to the hole if soil is poorly drained in winter.

2 Nip off the dead flower-spikes before they start to turn to seed, otherwise the whole plant tends to stop flowering.

3 If dotted through borders, thin out competitive neighbours or make a note to transplant to somewhere more open in spring.

4 Leave the old flower-spikes in place through winter as protection, then in early spring cut them down to the fresh green leaves at the base.

FAVOURITE VARIETIES

• *P. 'Sour Grapes'* – Bruised-purple mottled flowers.
• *P. 'Garnet'* – Lots of flowers in dark deep-red.
• *P. 'Firebird'* – Scarlet flowers and evergreen foliage.
• *P. 'Pink Endurance'* – Really long-flowering pink.

HEIGHT & SPREAD 50x50cm (18x18in) CLIMATE ZONES 9–10

TAKE CUTTINGS

In late summer, take 8cm (3in) long tips from side-shoots that aren't flowering. Remove the lower leaves from the bottom, and cut with a sharp knife just below a bud. Push them into pots or trays of moist, peat-free multipurpose compost and cover them with a clear plastic bag or cloche.

Don't let the cuttings dry out and transplant individually into 8cm (3in) pots when new leaves appear. Plant out in late spring the following year.

Penstemon 'Firebird' is an outstanding scarlet

While most **perennials** flower and fade, **penstemon** goes on right through summer and autumn. **Ideal** for filling **gaps.**

Michaelmas Daisy

Michaelmas daisies (*Aster*) provide a splash of colour when you need it most, just as the garden's starting to tire at the end of summer. Our favourites are *Aster ericoides* and *A. lateriflorus* 'Horizontalis' with their bushy clouds of tiny star-shaped flowers in autumn. For larger, more traditional daisies, the best is violet-blue *A. frikartii* 'Monch', which has an incredibly long flowering period, from summer right through into autumn. Group them together in drifts or as a snaking hedge through a border.

PLANT, LIFT AND DIVIDE

1 Plant in spring in well-drained, ordinary soil in sun. Stake with pea sticks, or garden centre-bought plastic hoops before the plant gets taller than 45cm (18in).

2 After flowering, the stems continue to look good, adding much-needed height and structure – even when plants have died down in winter, if they haven't flopped with the wet weather. Wait until late winter before cutting right down to the ground.

3 When clumps reach 45cm (18in) across, plants need to be lifted and divided in spring or they'll start to die out in the centre. Cut down the stems to the crown and dig them up with a spade. Place the clump on a flat piece of ground, push two garden forks back-to-back into the centre of the clump and lever the roots apart into pieces at least 20cm (8in) across.

PLAN FOR SPRING INTEREST

Asters are late starters and so need to be planted alongside a warm-up act for early summer. Bed out wallflowers (*see page 156*) around them for spring interest or with the silver-leaved perennial *Centaurea montana (left)*. A perennial cornflower, it flowers in early spring and can be cut to the ground in midsummer to make way for the Michaelmas daisies.

HEIGHT & SPREAD *Aster ericoides* and *A. lateriflorus* 'Horizontalis' 75x30cm (30x12in)

4 Replant in groups, 45cm (18in) apart, where they will flower later in the year.

They think it's all **over** ... but it's not! **Michaelmas daisies** take your garden into extra time, **flowering** from the end of summer right into **autumn.**

Aster frikatartii 'Monch' 70x40cm (28x16in) CLIMATE ZONES 2–4

Garden Chrysanthemum

If your idea of chrysanthemums is based on what comes cellophane-wrapped in supermarkets, then reconsider! The Rubellum hybrids are unsurpassable for colour in autumn and a real season extender, shining out through the rain and first of the frosts. They capture the season in their foliage and flowers colours, and as the leaves tint red with the cold, they exude a spicy, pungent scent that fills the air on fuggy autumn days. Classic varieties include the creamy 'Mary Stoker' and silvery-pink 'Clara Curtis'.

PLANT FOR LATE-SUMMER COLOUR

1 Early in the year, find your chrysanthemum a sunny corner with other autumn stalwarts, such as asters and late-flowering red hot pokers, where flowering won't be curtailed by the frosts.

2 Keep well watered in dry spells and feed occasionally with a balanced fertilizer until buds break.

3 Chrysanthemums are very prone to flopping when in flower and if they do they're ruined – so prevention is better than cure. Before they get to 45–60cm (18–24in), stake with pea sticks or by supporting the foliage with link stakes from the garden centre.

TIP

PINCH OUT TIPS

In early summer as growth starts to get away, pinch off the top 5–8cm (2–3in) of each shoot. Plants respond by becoming bushier, more flowery, less spindly and are less prone to flop in flower.

HEIGHT & SPREAD 75x50cm (30x20in) CLIMATE ZONE 6

Chrysanthemums can still be blooming in late autumn if you give them the sunny, cosy corner they deserve.

Chrysanthemum
'Clara Curtis' (ABOVE)
C. 'Mary Stoker' (RIGHT)

Grow Flowers for Cutting

If you want to have a plentiful supply of flowers for the house and the garden, the best plants to grow are annuals. From one pack of seed sown in spring you can gather hundreds of flowers all summer long. Don't be put off by the thought of growing plants from seed. All you need is some 8cm (3in) plastic pots, multipurpose compost and a porch or greenhouse to give them a flying start. Plant among existing border plants in sun, or better still, make your own mini cut-flower garden. Allocate a minimum 180x120cm (6x4ft) border for growing flowers, like vegetables in rows, perhaps surrounded by a low hazel picket for added harvest charm. The beauty of growing cut flowers from annuals is that the more you cut, the more you get, as cutting prevents plants going to seed.

HOW TO START OFF YOUR ANNUALS

1 Start seeds off in pots of moist compost in a greenhouse or porch in spring and sprinkle with water if the surface seems dry. Transfer seedlings into individual pots when about 2.5cm (1in) high. You only need about 6–10 of each plant for a plentiful harvest. (*See* page 24.)

2 Plant out after the frosts in late spring about 23cm (9in) apart in a weed-free, sunny spot and keep well watered. Also keep an eye out for slugs while plants are small.

TIP

HOW TO PICK
For the longest-lasting bunches, pick flowers when they are just opening and put them straight into a bucket of water, having stripped the stems of leaves. Gently shake off any pollen beetles and bugs first!

FIVE STARTER PLANTS FOR CUTTING

- **Marigold** – There are two main types – both easy – simple pot marigolds and the frilly French and African types which have striped or pom-pom petals. They are generally sunset shades of orange or yellow.
H 15–60cm (6–24in)

- **Cosmos** – Very quick to germinate, cosmos have soft feathery foliage and come in baby pinks, sexy scarlets and white. They flower from midsummer onwards.
H 90–120cm (3–4ft)

- **Cornflower** – A classic blue flower that performs best with repeated sowing through the summer, also available in white, pink and chocolate.
H 60–90cm (2–3ft)

- **Clary** – (ABOVE) A cottage garden favourite in pink, blues and purple, this salvia has flowers that dry on the stem to create everlasting flowers.
H 30–90cm (1–3ft) depending on variety.

- **Rudbeckia** – The annual rudbeckia comes in marmalade colours with a central brown cone. One of the best for flowering late into autumn. Choose varieties around 60–90cm (2–3ft) for cutting.

Artemisia

Marguerite

Pelargonium

Hosta

CHAPTER 6

Edgers and Softeners

Edgers and softeners spilling over the edges of patios and pathways will create a sense of abundance in your garden. Whether you choose them for their leaves or foamy flowers, they will build volume and effect. Foliage plants like heuchera make a vivid break from the usual greens, with purple or silvery-metallic leaves that either echo or contrast with the colours of nearby petals.

There are many cottage garden flowers here too, such as geraniums and catmint, that have sprawling stems that bustle round the feet of taller plants and hum with bees in summer.

For a more contemporary look, grasses soften edges and add movement to border surrounds and provide the opportunity to create your own meadow-style planting.

Purple-flowered *Geranium magnificum* lines a path leading to a potted *Hosta* 'Aureomarginata'

Artemisia

Artemisia 'Powis Castle' is the classic foliage shrub for hot, dry spots at the base of sunny walls. It's great as a frothy skirt to hide plants with skinny legs, such as shrub roses and standard topiary. Although it's evergreen don't expect too much in winter unless it's in a very sheltered spot, though it does come bouncing back every spring. Use it for silvery boulders in gravel, or in weaving lines like waves through borders. *Artemisia ludoviciana* is better for front of border or as a path-edger and is herbaceous – a welcome contrast to the mature greens of summer foliage.

FILL A SUNNY SPOT

1 Artemisia don't live long in unimproved heavy soils, preferring light, well-drained situations in full sun (they grow particularly well against south-facing brick walls). If your soil has a lot of clay in it, add a spade-full of grit and draw the soil into a mound before planting, so excess water drains away from the roots.

2 The foliage of Artemisia 'Powis Castle' gets tatty in winter. Cut back in spring to encourage fresh, bushy leaves. Do this as soon as new growth sprouts from the base.

3 A. *ludoviciana* dies down completely in winter and can be cut off at ground level as soon as the stems look untidy.

PESTS

WATCH FOR BLACKFLY
Blackfly love Artemisia 'Powis Castle', sucking the sap from new shoots and slowing its growth. Look out for them in spring, clustered around the fresh tips in dense patches. If there are only a few, spray with an organic soft soap spray from the garden centre, or blast them with water from the hosepipe, while gently rubbing off the pest with your fingers. If you keep doing it, you'll gradually get rid of them. Where infestations are large, snip off the growing tips and dispose of in the council green bin or your compost heap. Look over the plant carefully so as not to miss any clusters and spray with a jet of water from your hosepipe to disrupt any new infestations.

HEIGHT & SPREAD 60x90cm (24x36in) CLIMATE ZONES A. 'Powis Castle' 8; *A. ludoviciana* 5

Artemisia 'Powis Castle' at home in a gravel garden (LEFT), and perennial *Artemisia ludoviciana* (INSET BELOW)

An **essential shrub** for the dry gravel garden, **artemisia** is a shining example of a plant that doesn't need flowers to look **fabulous**.

Hardy Geranium

Geraniums are very popular perennials, and justly so because they're real troupers – unfussy about soil and able to grow in a whole range of difficult situations. The trick is getting the right one for the job as there are varieties for hot sun, for deep shade, gravel, and growing with grasses in meadows. A few, like *Geranium* 'Rozanne', flower for a long time and live in sun or part-shade; others, like *G. endressii* and *G. macrorrhizum*, spread to cover dry hard-to-plant ground in shade, while *G. cinereum* and varieties positively revel and self-sow in sun-baked gravel.

FOR SUN

As flowering comes to an end and stems get leggy, shear back to the base for a fresh surge of growth for late summer.

Geranium renardii – A compact mound-forming plant for front of border. Its lovely foliage is joined by small white flowers in early summer. The blue variety 'Phillippe Vapelle' flowers for longer. H&S 25x30cm (10x12in)

Geranium pratense 'Mrs Kendall Clark' – This hazy-blue classic of meadow cranesbill prefers moist fertile soil. Cut it back to the ground if it gets mildew (powdery-white leaves) in late summer. H&S 60x30cm (24x12in)

Geranium 'Johnson's Blue' – One of the best for blue flowers, it starts flowering in late spring and has its main flush in summer. Divide it regularly to keep it fresh and full of blooms.
H&S 40x50cm (12x20in)

Geraniums are plants with a purpose and can be **set to work** in the **hardest-to-plant** parts of the garden.

FOR SHADE

Geranium phaeum 'Samobor' – All *phaeum* thrive in deep dry shade, although they do grow in sun too. They have beaked purple-black flowers in early summer. This variety has interesting chocolate-splotched leaves that tint yellow in autumn. In borders cut the plant down to the ground as soon as it starts to look tatty in midsummer and it'll quickly flush with fresh leaves again.
H&S 50x60cm (20x24in)

Geranium macrorrhizum – Makes weed-suppressing ground cover in sun or deep shade with white, pink or magenta flowers. The foliage tints in the cold and it has pungently aromatic leaves.
H&S 30x30cm (12x12in)

TIP

HOW TO DIVIDE GERANIUMS

Spreading geraniums can get a bit bald in the middle after a few years, so you need to lift and divide them. In spring or autumn, dig up the clump of roots, place it on a flat surface and then divide it into dinnerplate-sized portions. Do this by placing garden forks back to back and levering them apart. Freshen up the soil with compost before replanting the divisions, and use the extras as swaps with friends or use to brighten up other tricky spots.

Ornamental Grasses

It took a while for gardeners to get to know what to do with ornamental grasses. When interest first started to grow in the early 1990s, they were always grouped together, whether they were tall, small, herbaceous or evergreen, in large clumps. But now it's as if they're seen as individuals and grown to look good amongst flowers in borders.

Generally speaking, grasses prefer sun and a light well-drained soil, tending to perish in heavy clays, although there are a few exceptions (*see opposite*). Late spring is the best time to plant. On heavy soils, plant in containers or in raised beds with plenty of grit added for drainage.

WAYS TO PLANT

Their look is far more sophisticated than the suburban pampas grass planted as a specimen in a lawn. Tall *Miscanthus* with its arching green ribbons is great for tropical borders with canna lilies, while *Stipa* and *Calamagrostis* complement roses and herbaceous plants, from early summer to the late daisies. Evergreens look good in winter, while deciduous types needn't be chopped down until early spring, adding height with their skeletal white stems, like ghosts of summer past.

HOW TO PRUNE

How you prune a grass is all down to how far it dies back for winter. What you're trying to avoid is last year's dried-out growth detracting from the new fresh-green blades, which will happen if you leave cutting back too late. Only grasses that die back should be cut back though because the shock can kill others, and they just need a spruce-up in early spring.

Comb out – Use a spring-tine rake (or failing that, your fingers) to gently ease out last year's spent flower-spikes, keeping the leaves intact. Do this with *Festuca, Carex, Stipa arundinacea* and *S. tenuissima*.

Cut down to the ground – For grasses that die back completely to ground level, cut back the dried stems to the ground with secateurs in early spring. Do this with *Miscanthus, Pennisetum, Phalaris* and *Molinia*.

Cut down to 'hedgehogs' – This is for plants where new growth starts in early spring as a green tuft amongst last year's foliage, so shear down to spiky 20cm (8in) clumps to keep the base of young leaves intact. Do this with *Calamagrostis, Stipa calamagrostis* and *Deschampsia*.

CLIMATE ZONES *Miscathus sinensis* 4; *Stipa arundinacea* 8; *Calamagrostis* 7

WHAT TO BUY

• *Calamagrostis* 'Karl Foerster' –
The one to plant for heavy clay, a
very upright grass with mushroom-
pink flowers, turning silver into
autumn. Cut down to hedgehogs
in early spring.
H&S 120x60cm (4x2ft)

• *Stipa calamagrostis* – Lovely with
lilies and roses, where its arching
growth benefits from the support
of its neighbours. Gold feather-duster
flowers from early spring into autumn.
Cut to hedgehogs in early spring.
H&S 90x60cm (3x2ft)

• *Stipa tenuissima* – One of the
best for dry soil in sun, with bronzy
leaves that persist through winter
and flowers like a mane of waving
golden hair from early spring right
through winter. Tidy up in spring by
combing out.
H&S 60x60cm (2x2ft)

• *Miscanthus sinensis* – Good on dry
ground as long as you look after them
when young. All varieties are elegant
with feathery tassels held on spear-
like stems.
M. 'Morning Light' has variegated
leaves that redden in autumn;
M. 'Silberfeder' is very tall and
elegant and good for back of border.
For tropical borders go for *M.
sacchariflorus* or smaller striped
M. s. 'Strictus', which has leaves
banded with cream. Cut to ground
level in late winter.
H&S 1–2mx60cm (3–6½x2ft)

• *Stipa arundinacea* – Evergreen
self-sowing grass for good soil in sun
or part-shade. The rolls of leaves turn
bronze in midwinter when it looks
best. Comb out in winter.
H&S 60x90cm (2x3ft)

**Calamagrostis 'Karl
Foerster'** (LEFT),
Stipa arundinacea (ABOVE)

Grasses hold sway in the late
summer garden, with quivering seedheads
that shimmer in the low, warm
harvest sunshine.

Stipa tenuissima (RIGHT)
M. sinensis 'Variegatus' (FAR RIGHT)

Heuchera

Heuchera is a perennial foliage plant that doesn't die down in winter, so it's interesting all year round. Large-leaved varieties like the deep red 'Plum Pudding' make a great contrast at the front of the border with all the greens, while more compact types, such as 'Chocolate Ruffles', are ideal for pots. The subtle, foamy wands of white or red flowers are a bonus in early summer but their real beauty comes to the fore in autumn and winter when little else is performing.

PLANTING AND CARE

1 Knock plants out of their pots and you'll see that each bunch of leaves grows up from a slightly woody trunk. Bury this when planting, ideally in light shade and moist soil, so everything below the pen on the picture is below soil level. It roots easily, and the plant looks better when well anchored in this way.

2 In late winter, as new leaves are coming through, tidy up the plant by trimming off the oldest leaves down to the base with secateurs.

3 Plants over three years old can develop quite long woody bases, particularly if they're growing in dry soil. In early autumn, dig up plants, and divide with your fingers. Then replant the pieces, burying the roots as for step 1. Water in well.

HEIGHT & SPREAD 40x40cm (16x16in) CLIMATE ZONE 5

Heuchera 'Palace Purple'
(RIGHT) **and**
H. 'Beauty Colour' (BELOW)

USE IN WINTER POTS

If heathers and conifers aren't your style, heuchera are the ideal evergreen alternative. Combine with pansies or violas for buckets of cottage garden charm. Plants can survive for a few years in the same pot, continuing on even when winter bedding like pansies are replaced with summer partners of marigolds or Cape daisies. Pot up using a peat-free multipurpose compost.

Heuchera are the new hosta – they have **fantastic foliage**, pretty flowers, are **great** for **pots**, and slugs don't touch them!

Hosta

Hostas are fabulous perennials for the shade, looking extravagant and lush from the moment they burst from the soil in spring to when their leaves die down in autumn. But for slugs, hostas are manna from heaven, and growing them is largely about protecting them from these slimy, hole-punchers. Well-grown plants have bold leaves that enrich borders filled with run-of-the-mill foliage, and the variegated types do wonders to lift gloomy shade. Large-leaved varieties, such as blue *Hosta sieboldiana elegans*, add architectural elegance or a focal point.

PLANT AND PROTECT

1 Slugs will go to any length to get at your hostas, even hitching a ride on the base of pots from the garden centre. Delay planting at your peril, as it's a myth that hostas are safe in pots. The moment you get home, protect plants with a sprinkle of organic slug pellets, taking care to keep them away from the leaves. This should keep them in check, but hosta collectors scrape away and replace the top inch of topsoil from around plants to remove any slug eggs.

2 Plant in spring or autumn in any moisture-retentive soil. Dig in plenty of compost or well-rotted manure, and if the soil is dry, add some wetted moisture-retaining granules to the planting holes, forking them into the base. You buy these in sachets from garden centres and they are generally used in pots and hanging baskets. In their dry form, they're like sugar crystals, but once wet they swell into a jelly and act like a sponge, holding a reservoir of water around roots. Always soak crystals before planting.

3 For plants growing in pots, protect leaves from slugs and snails with a barrier of copper tape stuck just under the rim. Don't allow lower leaves to create a bridge over the tape on to the foliage. Design-wise, plant one variety per container as they look best uncluttered and use half-and-half soil-based John Innes No.2 and multicompost with a handful of added grit for drainage. Give a monthly liquid feed with a balanced liquid fertilizer or fortify by putting slow-release pellets into the pot each spring.

HEIGHT & SPREAD 30x30–75cm (12x12–30in) CLIMATE ZONES 4–7

COLOUR CO-ORDINATE FOR THE SITE

Hostas come in different leaf colours and the shade of the foliage dictates where it must be grown.

For full sun, choose green or yellow-leaved types which tend to go a dirty green in low light.

In dappled shade, go for blues, as they can scorch in sun, and the variegated types with white or yellow stripes.

During the growing season, feed by scattering chicken manure pellets around the plants or mulch with manure in winter just prior to leaves coming up.

Hosta 'Halcyon' revels in heavy clay and deep shade (RIGHT)

Hostas are plant magnets, drawing the eye towards their bold and colourful outlines, giving dull borders instant charisma.

Marguerite

Marguerites (*Argyranthemum frutescens*) are sold along with other tender patio plants like petunias and Cape daisies, but there's more to these plants than just summer bedding. Cool and elegant, they add a classical touch to planters and are really hard-working. They're covered in white daisies from early summer to autumn and though not hardy outdoors, can be kept alive if brought indoors in a frost-free greenhouse from year to year without too much fuss to become long-term, fair-weather friends.

PROVIDE PERMANENT BLOOMS

1 After frosts finish, plant out in a sunny, well-drained, front or mid-border position, either in the soil or in containers filled with 50/50 soil-based and multipurpose compost. They're largely pest-free, but watch out for aphids on the tips in early summer. Spray with soft soap or wash off with water.

2 Deadhead with scissors or secateurs regularly, taking the flower-stem back to the nearest leaves.

3 In late summer, take cuttings by snipping 8cm (3in) long shoots (preferably without flowers, or remove buds). Cut off the leaves from the bottom half of the cutting and push into a gritty, moist, multipurpose compost. Keep moist in the greenhouse or on a warm windowsill indoors until new leaves appear within a couple of weeks. Then pot on into individual pots and keep frost-free until planting out the following spring. By the summer, you should have a bushy, 50cm (20in) tall plant.

HEIGHT & SPREAD 75x75cm (30x30in) CLIMATE ZONE 9

HOW TO GROW IN POTS

Marguerites are trouble-free pot plants, more drought-tolerant than most, so good for a sunny hot spot. Feed once a fortnight with a balanced liquid fertilizer through summer. If you have space indoors or in the greenhouse you don't even have to take cuttings to keep from year to year as pots can simply be stowed out of the worst of the cold.

Bring the container into a porch or conservatory where it'll carry on flowering, alternatively keep it in an unheated greenhouse and then water sparingly through winter. It'll look pretty sorry for itself until spring when you can give it a good water and a feed with a slow-release fertilizer. Prune back to healthy new growth when leaves start to grow and it will flower in time for summer.

Marguerites make long-term patio plants if you have room to store them in a porch or a frost-free greenhouse during the winter

Like fluffy clouds, marguerites float above borders and pots, billowing with daisies all summer long.

Nepeta

Nepeta (or catmint) flowers for a very long time, from early summer to autumn, with soft silvery leaves and foamy blue flowers. It's *the* plant for softening path edges and tumbling over low walls and an essential choice for dry sandy soils where plants run to seed all too quickly. Try *Nepeta* 'Six Hills Giant' under classical statuary – the purple haze at its white feet has the same effect as a smoke machine – adding a touch of mystery. *N. racemosa* 'Walker's Low' is smaller, but has the best blue for borders. Both attract bees, but if you want a plant for Felix to enjoy, choose *N.* x *faassenii* – cats can't get enough of it!

HOW TO GROW

1 Plant in full sun in well-drained soil in spring. Small plants grow very quickly, sprawling to 60cm (2ft) in the first summer, but if your soil is well-drained there's no harm in planting in autumn, as here with *Rudbeckia fulgida sullivantii* 'Goldsturm'.

2 By summer, the first flush of blue flowers will be over and you'll be left with the purple flower-cases. These can be quite attractive in their own right, but if you trim off the flower-spikes, it'll bounce back within a few weeks with fresh foliage and more flowers for the rest of summer.

3 If your plant edges a lawn, it'll get in the way of the mower when you cut. To avoid the powerful temptation of rolling the mower over the top, peg the nepeta out of the way with a couple of bamboo canes before you start.

HEIGHT & SPREAD *Nepeta* 'Six Hills Giant' 90x90cm (36x36in); *N.* 'Walker's Low' 75x60cm (30x24in)

The brilliant blue of *Nepeta racemosa* 'Walker's Low' makes an attractive border for a low wall. (BELOW)

If you're looking for a plant to surround the base of a statue or sunny bench, you can't beat nepeta.

GIVE CATS A TREAT!

Female, and some male, cats are irresistibly drawn to the aroma of nepeta foliage, as its active ingredient turns cats on! They respond by rolling on it and dribbling all over it – it's apparently a genetic response to a dominant female and not all cats have the gene. Of course, it doesn't do the plant a lot of good, but fortunately the one they're most attracted to is *N. x faassenii*, so it's the one to avoid if there are lots of neighbourhood cats. But if you want to give your cat a treat, grow this one and bag up sprigs in sachets for special home-grown Christmas presents.

Pelargonium

If you're looking for something to soften your pots or edge the patio, you can't beat pelargoniums. Our favourites are the fancy-leaf species, which are drought-tolerant with soft, furry, aromatic leaves and dainty flowers. Many are very old varieties with charming names, like the salmon-flowered and cream-edged *Pelargonium* 'Frank Headley' or the easy, doily-leaved *P.* 'Concolor Lace' or two-toned *P.* 'Tip-Top Duet'. For unusual fragrance, try rose-scented *P.* 'Attar of Roses' or lemony *P.* 'Mabel Grey'. but they need to be overwintered in the house or conservatory.

1 Buy in pots in spring. They're available as plug plants (*see* page 13) or in flower in spring in 10cm (3in) pots. Both need protecting from frost indoors on a windowsill or in a cold greenhouse. Pot plugs on into 10cm (3in) pots as soon as you get them home, pinch out any flowers to encourage plants to root and grow larger. Water both pots and plugs sparingly, letting the compost dry out before you water them again.

2 Once frosts finish, plant out in the garden in pots or borders. They're unfussy so long as soil is well-drained and they get plenty of sun. Feed plants in pots with a high-potash tomato feed through the summer and don't let compost dry out completely.

TIPS

EASY CUTTINGS

Taking cuttings from pelargoniums is child's play and it's the best way to keep cherished plants through the winter. With a sharp knife snip 10cm (3in) shoots just below a bud. Ideally shoots should be without flowers, but if so then cut any off. Remove all but the top set of leaves by snapping off between finger and thumb. Push three cuttings around the edge of a 10cm (3in) pot filled with a half-and-half mix of moist horticultural grit and peat-free multipurpose compost. Keep the pot on an indoor windowsill out of direct sunlight and water when the surface of the compost dries out. In early spring, knock cuttings out of pots, separate the roots and plant each one separately into 12cm (5in) pots. Then put outdoors after the frosts.

HEIGHT & SPREAD 30x30cm (12x12in) CLIMATE ZONE 10

3 Deadhead by snapping off the spent flower-stalks at the point where they're attached to the stem to keep new flowers coming.

Pelargoniums are the most tolerant bedding plant of all, flowering continuously right through the summer.

Pelargonium 'TipTop Duet' has two-tone flowers (ABOVE), while *P.* 'Concolor' (INSET) has small ones, but the scent from the leaves is delicious

Sedum

Some things in life are hard to improve on, and *Sedum* 'Autumn Joy' is one. Although it's been around for a long time, there isn't another variety to match its year-round good looks. Although a perennial which dies down, its tweedy russet flower-stalks shrug off the weather even in winter. Unlike most late bloomers, the silver-blue foliage is a feature in its own right even in dry soils and hot summers. It flowers right through from summer into autumn, with dusky pink cushions that make an irresistible landing pad for butterflies.

GROW A YEAR-ROUND ATTRACTION

1 Plant in sun and well-drained soil. Like many autumn bloomers, they can look a little lost on their own. But plant a few in a wavy line through a border and it'll create the illusion of a full-flowering garden even if everything else has finished.

Sedum are really easy to propagate from divisions in spring, so even if you don't want to splash out on lots of plants all at once, you can gradually build up the effect with cuttings over a relatively short period of time.

2 On older plants, flowers tend to flop, leaving the crown exposed, like a monk's head, with a great bald patch in the middle. A quick trick to stop it happening is to loosely tie the heavy heads together with twine, halfway up the flower-stem where it won't be seen. Make a note to lift and divide the plant the following spring.

3 Leave the flowerheads on the plant until late winter and cut down to the new foliage at the base before it all starts to grow again in spring.

TIPS

BRING IN BUTTERFLIES

Butterflies are drawn to the nectar at the base of certain flowers, and each flowerhead of sedum is made up of hundreds of tiny blooms, hence its appeal. They also like to bask in the same sort of heat as sedum itself. But to guarantee butterflies in your garden you have to give them not just food for the adults, but also food for the caterpillars. You'll be glad to hear this doesn't involve ornamental flowering plants, but plain old stinging nettles. Leave a patch in a corner of your garden to encourage butterflies to lay their eggs.

HEIGHT & SPREAD 60x60cm (2x2ft) CLIMATE ZONE 5

Sedum 'Autumn Joy' is like a fine wine mellowing through the summer from a fruity rose pink to a deep, rich claret.

Create an Annual Meadow

The swaying flowers and sun-bleached grass of a wildflower meadow are a look that most gardeners covet. The problem is that very few of us have the right soil for authentic grassland plants as the beds and borders in the average back garden are too rich for their delicate appetites.

Wildflowers thrive in impoverished conditions where thuggish grasses and weeds can't get the upper hand. So, if you want a little piece of cornfield in your borders, you've got to pick from a pallet of plants that will enjoy a hearty clay soil or even your compost-filled borders and are easy to look after. Best of all, they can be sown from inexpensive packets of seed in spring.

HOW TO SOW FROM SEED IN SPRING

1 In early spring, sow grass seed, such as quaking grass, into trays of moist seed-sowing compost. Trays are good for the grasses because they are large enough for lots of plants. Sow flowers, such as poppies or marigolds, into 5cm (2in) pots.

2 When plants are large enough to handle, move them individually into their own 5cm (2in) pots of multipurpose compost. Poppies dislike having their roots disturbed when planting, so either prick out into peat pots which can be planted directly into the ground, or make your own biodegradable pots from cones of newspaper.

3 Plant out in a sunny border when plants fill the pots. Set out the grasses first in a loose chequerboard, then put the flowers in the gaps, spreading them in drifts between the grasses for that natural look. Water well and you'll be enjoying them all summer.

THE PLANTS

● *Stipa tenuissima* – Soft, short-lived, perennial, evergreen with bronze leaves turning blonde through winter. H&S 60x30cm (24x12in)

● Hare's tail (*Lagurus ovatus*) – Easy annual grass with fluffy white seedheads. H&S 45x20cm (18x9in)

● Pot marigold (*Calendula officinalis*) – striking yellow or orange cottage garden flower, keep deadheading for a long display. H&S 60x30cm (24x12in)

● Quaking grass (*Briza maxima*) – Easy annual grass with fluttering wheat-like seedheads. H&S 45x20cm (18x9in)

● Ladybird poppy (*Papaver commutatum*) – Glossy red poppy with black central splotches. H&S 45x12cm (18x4in)

TIP

There's no need to buy the seeds again, you can collect them for re-sowing in late summer; alternatively you can let them self-sow where they are. There should be plenty to re-stock your garden with enough left over for the birds to enjoy too! *Stipa tenuissima* is perennial, while everything else will self-sow and come up again.

Daffodil

Snowdrop

Viola

CHAPTER 7

Flower Carpets

Flower carpet plants are traditionally the last thing you plant after the shrubs, perennials and trees have gone in. This mixture of bulbs and bedding planted *en masse* vastly improves a garden, painting it with sheets of colour early in the year. Think of carpet plants as embellishers, a fine winter coat for your borders, forgotten about in the summer but so welcome once the weather turns chilly.

These are tough plants too, occupying the spaces between other bigger plants and thriving in tricky places, under trees and near walls. Design-wise, they have a natural romance, nostalgic of a walk through woods and the best of the countryside. So the only rule when planting is: don't hold back. Use them in sweeps through your borders or literally paint with them, making interesting shapes and swirls through lawns.

Lovely native daffodils, *Narcissus pseudonarcissus*, with *Chionodoxa*

Anemone

Crocus

Anemone

Anemones flower when it's still cold in early spring, cheerfully defying the weather. They're small but their glossy petals glow in the sun and catch the eye. If they're happy, they spread to become a satin sheet over the soil. The most common types are the purpley-blue *Anemone blanda* 'Blue Shades' and the snow-white *A.* 'White Splendour'. They look best weaving through other plants in sun or semi-shade and under shrubs – a must-have plant for a woodland garden.

MAKE A SPRING CARPET

1 In spring, buy pot-grown plants and place into soil enriched with garden compost and leafmould. This makes them feel at home as they love woodland soils. They're great edgers for borders and paths where they will spread.

2 Mulch around the plant with more compost, 1cm (½ in) thick, to encourage the plant to establish from seed too. As plants die down beneath the soil like bulbs after flowering, it's a good idea to mark their position so you can't accidentally dig them up. Peg a hoop of wire around the clumps to mark their position and press it down into the mulch. It's out of sight, but will stop your trowel before any damage is done.

GROW FROM TUBERS

For planting large areas, tubers are the most economical option. Look out for them in the bulb section of the garden centre in autumn. Before planting, soak in a saucer of water overnight to rehydrate the dried-out tubers and give them a good start. Plant just below the surface, about 1cm (½ in) deep and 10cm (4in) apart.

Anemone blanda makes a carpet of purple-blue daisies in spring, giving the base of borders a touch of woodland charm (RIGHT AND ABOVE)

HEIGHT & SPREAD 10x10cm (4x4in) CLIMATE ZONES 5–8

Anemones do a great job of making spring yellows more **interesting** – a brilliant **complement** to the first **daffodils** and **primroses**.

Daffodil

Daffodils (*Narcissus*) are so undemanding it's no surprise that most gardens contain a few, but for sustained flowering you need to plant a number of varieties that bloom at different times. For the earliest colour, plant *Narcissus* 'February Gold', which flowers throughout spring. For mid spring go for a traditional trumpet like *N.* 'Dutch Master', then follow on with sweetly scented jonquils and miniatures such as *N. pseudo-narcissus*, ideal for naturalizing on banks and grass. Finally, for late spring, plant the pale *N. poeticus* types that look best in drifts around trees.

PLANT DRIFTS OF BULBS

1 For the widest selection buy and plant bulbs in autumn rather than use expensive pot-grown plants in spring. To plant naturally in grass, the best way to position the bulbs (and the most fun!) is to throw them in the air and plant where they land. This randomizes their spacing just as it would be if they were wild. Through borders, snake drifts between plants to create a river of colour at flowering time.

2 Plant bulbs 10cm (4in) deep making sure the base of each bulb touches the bottom of the hole – as any air pockets beneath it will inhibit growth. Then fill back over with soil.

3 After flowering take off fading blooms to encourage the production of flowers for next year. If you've got too many to do by hand, swipe them off with a bamboo cane.

The down side of daffodils is their fading foliage, which can look tatty. You have two choices: wait for a minimum of five weeks after flowering, then cut down with secateurs (or mow, if in grass), or dig up plants carefully and replant somewhere out of the way (old window boxes are good). Keep watered until the foliage dies down and replant in the flowering position in autumn.

Large trumpet daffodils like pale *Narcissus* 'Ice Follies' and golden *N.* 'Carlton' make easy grow-your-own cut flowers

BEST FOR POTS

All daffodils can be grown in pots, but the best are the jonquils and miniatures like *Narcissus bulbocodium* and the amusingly named *N. canaliculatus* as this raises up their dainty, sweetly scented flowers to where they can be enjoyed.

Plant bulbs 12cm (5in) deep in pots arranged 2.5cm (1in) apart. Cover the bulbs with peat-free multipurpose compost and then place another layer of bulbs over the top – this will give you two staged flushes of flowers.

Keep outside and they'll flower at the normal time or leave in the greenhouse for early flowers. Keep the compost moist and feed as soon as the bulbs are in growth. Always repot your bulbs every two years.

Daffodils aren't just for Easter, if you choose carefully, you can have flowers from spring until summer.

Snowdrop

Tiny knights in white, snowdrops (*Galanthus*) will rescue your garden from the grips of winter depression. They flower for a few weeks in early spring when the weather is at its worst, heroically filling that gap before the first cheery daffodils appear. If you don't get out into your garden much in winter, remember to pick a few so you can admire their exquisite markings at close quarters.

THE NATURAL LOOK

Amazingly, given the tiny differences between snowdrops, there are over 100 varieties, making them real collectors' plants. But if you want to keep it simple, then go for the most natural one, *Galanthus nivalis*. It makes snowy swathes beneath trees or through borders, or for plumper flowers shaped like hooped petticoats try the double-flowered G. 'Flore Pleno'.

1 In late winter, plant in the green, in other words, when the bulbs are in leaf either as garden centre-bought pots or clumps from friends. Snowdrops like dappled shade, but neither extreme shade nor strong summer sunshine. Cluster them under trees, shrubs or on lightly shaded banks with winter aconites, crocus and oriental hellebores for a succession of spring colour.

2 The following winter, make new snowdrops for free, by lifting and dividing clumps after flowering ends. Dig a little bit deeper than trowel depth to avoid snapping leaves from bulbs. Split into groups of three bulbs and replant 10–12cm (4–5in) deep, adding a trowel-full of leafmould or garden compost. Next year, each new patch will be bigger as bulbs multiply.

HEIGHT & SPREAD 15x8cm (6x3in) CLIMATE ZONE 8 and above

One of the **joys** of snowdrops is that you can plant them in **flower** and instantly make **winter** a far **better** place to be!

Galanthus nivalis (LEFT)
Snowdrops naturalize easily and look terrific with winter-flowering aconites (ABOVE)

TIP

COVER DIFFICULT SLOPES
Snowdrops love sloping north-facing banks, so are the perfect winter cover for awkward-to-plant inclines. If you have a shady slope, an easy planting plan would be native primroses (*Primula vulgaris*), evergreen silver euonymus, and the odd patch of euphorbia, underplanted with lots of snowdrops. Euphorbia spreads, so keep it in place by thinning out the edges occasionally.

Viola

In look and size, violas are somewhere between the tiny native violet and the bedding pansy. Not scented like the violet, nor so gaudy as the pansy, they have an old-fashioned cottage garden look and are great for pots or borders. They flush with flowers in spring, stop for the hottest weeks of summer and come again for autumn. The kinds you buy in the polystyrene packs at the garden centre are short-lived (a year or two at most). If you want a plant that will set up a permanent home in your borders, look out for heartsease (*Viola tricolor*) and *V. cornuta*.

BUY IN SPRING OR AUTUMN

1 Buy violas as pot plants or in polystyrene packs in autumn or early spring and plant either along the edges of borders, under roses or in containers. Space 15cm (6in) apart in the ground, closer in winter pots as they won't grow much when it's cold.

2 If you want to collect seeds, wait until the seedheads burst open into a star, then pick the whole stem. Scrape off the seed and press straight into a pot of sowing compost. Don't cover the seeds. In summer and autumn, seedlings will come up within the week and can be potted on into individual pots for planting out in autumn or spring.

3 Sometimes border plants run out of steam in midsummer and get straggly. Revive them by shearing back to a few centimetres above soil level. Water well afterwards and they'll quickly bounce back into flower once it's cooler. This is also a good way of dealing with mildew.

HEIGHT & SPREAD 15–20cm (4–6in) CLIMATE ZONES 6–9

Violas have the friendliest faces of all flowers and love to mingle with neighbouring plants.

Bedding viola come in pale blues and tangerine (ABOVE), or go for the old favourite heartsease, *Viola tricolor* (RIGHT)

TIP

LOOK OUT FOR MILDEW

Powdery mildew shows up on stems, leaves and flowers as a fine white coating. It occurs in hot, dry conditions, so patio pots are particularly prone, as are plants in hot border positions. It's not really worth trying to save pot annuals — you may as well replace with other new plants.

Wallflower

Wallflowers (*Erysimum*) have a fuddy-duddy reputation thanks to their use by parks' departments as the stiff biennial backbone in regimental spring bedding schemes. But there are more natural ways to use wallflowers, such as planting at the base of a wall or mingling with herbaceous plants in a border. Planted informally they make a carpet of early colour in spicy mauves, oranges and yellows that start in spring and continue into early summer. They have a sweet fragrance too and look great with daffodils and evergreen grasses.

PLANT IN AUTUMN

1 Buy wallflowers in bundles from the garden centre in autumn. Don't be put off by the fact they're bare-root (not potted up) but do cut them out of their ties and get them straight into the ground or a bucket of water as soon as you get home.

2 Plant in drifts among herbaceous plants, which will make room for the wallflowers as they die down for winter. This is a good technique for creating a succession of colour, with the herbaceous plants following the wallflowers. They also look fresh and modern combined with small evergreen grasses such as *Stipa tenuissima*. Alternatively, go traditional and mingle them amongst daffodils and electric blue hyacinths.

3 By early summer, plants are flopping and going to seed, so pull them out, roots and all, and put on the compost heap.

OR SOW FROM SEED

If you want more choice about colour, you can sow wallflowers from seed in summer. You can either sow direct into the ground in lines, then transplant to where they're going to flower, or sow in pots. They're easy, come up fast and are the right size for planting out in autumn (*see page 24*).

HEIGHT & SPREAD 45x30cm (18x12in) CLIMATE ZONES 3–8

No other plant has the **range** of **summery** colours or makes so much **impact** in early **spring.**

HOLES IN THE LEAVES

Flea beetle love wallflowers as they're members of the cabbage family. Damage looks like tiny pinprick holes in leaves. The pest is more of a problem with summer-sown seedlings and the best way to deal with it is by prevention. Cover seedlings with horticultural fleece until plants are 30cm (12in) tall. More mature plants can cope with minor infestations without it affecting the flowering.

Wallflowers with *Stipa tenuissima* and perennial cornflowers in late spring (ABOVE)

Glossary

These are some basic terms that appear throughout the text.

Annual – a plant that lives out its life in a year. This means that it will grow from seed, flower and set more seed in a single growing season. Most bedding plants like busy lizzies and petunias fall into this category.

Biennial – a plant that grows leaves in its first year and flowers in its second year such as foxgloves.

Balanced fertilizer – a plant food with equal amounts of the main plant nutrients (nitrogen, phosphates and potassium) that encourages leaves, roots and flowers to grow equally.

Compost – in gardening, compost is a name for two things:
1. The stuff that comes in bags from the garden centre that plants are potted into, consisting of either sterilized soil, peat or coir.
2. Decomposed lawn clippings, stems and leaves that are used for soil improving and mulching.

Corm – a bulb-like root as found on crocus and crocosmia.

Deciduous – the term given to plants that lose their leaves for winter and re-grow new ones each spring.

Double-flowered – flowers with two or more layers of petals.

Dieback – when shoot tips die and become twiggy, as often seen on unhealthy roses.

Germination – the action of a seed when it begins to grow into a plant.

Hardy – plants that survive cold and frosty weather in winter. The opposite of this is tender.

Herbaceous – plants that die down for winter and re-emerge in spring.

Toby Buckland and his wife Lisa share the gardening tasks at home

Often used in the phrase 'herbaceous perennial' and translates as summer flowers.

Horticultural grit – crushed angular stone 2–4mm (¼–½in) in diameter often mixed into potting compost or soil to improve drainage or as a decorative and slug-deterring mulch on the top of pots.

Loam-based – composts that have sterilized soil as their main ingredient. This makes them richer and closer to good garden soils than peat, bark and coir-based composts.

Mulch – a layer of bark, garden compost or stone chippings spread between plants, to either enrich the soil, hold in moisture or prevent weeds from growing.

Multipurpose compost – a bagged compost that is suitable for seed sowing, potting and striking cuttings. Usually the core constituent is peat.

Native – a plant that grows naturally in a particular place, as opposed to one introduced from another environment.

Naturalizing – encouraging a bulb or a plant to colonize an area as they would in the wild. For example, snowdrops and foxgloves allowed to self-sow and grow where they want.

Nematodes – microscopic worm-like organisms that naturally occur in the soil and water. There are thousands of types – a few are pests while some are used to predate plant pests, like slugs. They are part of the relatively new organic technology developed as an alternative to chemicals and referred to as 'biological control'.

Overwinter – keeping a plant frost free in a greenhouse or in the house.

Perennial – a plant that lives for two or more years.

PH – refers to how alkaline or acidic soil is: below 7 is acidic, 7 is neutral, above 7 is alkaline.

Pinching out – removing the growing tip of a young plant to enourage lots of side shoots. This is a technique used on annuals like cosmos to make them bushier and more flowery.

Plug plants – baby plants (seedlings or rooted cuttings) sold in spring for pots and baskets.

Rhizome – root-like underground stem, as found on bearded iris and canna lilies.

Rootball – the soil held around the plants roots and what you handle when a plant is dug from the ground or knocked from its pot.

Single flowered – plants with a single set of petals that look simple (as opposed to double).

Slow-release pellet – a type of fertilizer which releases food to the plant through the whole growing season, unlike liquid fertilizers, which offer an immediate hit.

Species – plants that have the same general characteristics.

Standard – a plant trained to have a clear stem to make a lollipop shape.

Topiary – any plant, usually evergreen, which has been clipped into a shape.

Variegated – refers to leaves with paler, usually cream or white, markings.

Vine eyes – a screw with a hooped end ideal for fixing wires to a wall or fence.

Water-retaining gel – crystals sold in sachets which swell up like pieces of jelly and are for mixing with soil and compost to hold extra water around plant roots.

Well-drained – refers to compost or soil that allows water to percolate through so soil never stagnates and becomes waterlogged.

Well-rotted manure – horse, cow or pig dung which has decomposed over a year, so has lost its smell and is the perfect consistency for feeding plants and improving soil.

Index

Main entries are given in **bold** type, illustrations in *italic*.

Acer palmatum **40–1**
 A.p. dissectum 40
 A.p. dissectum
  'Inaba-shidare' 41
Agapanthus **56–7**
 A. africanus 56, *57*
 A. Headbourne hybrids 56
Alcea **88–9**
 A. filicifolia 89
 A. rosea 88
 A.r. 'Nigra' 88, *89*
Allium **54–5**
 A. 'Globemaster' 54
 A. 'Purple Sensation' 54, *55*
Anemone *(blanda)* 147, **148–9**
 A.b. 'Blue Shades' 148, *148–9*
 A.b. 'White Splendour' 148
Anthemis 'Sauce Hollandaise'
 139
Aquilegia *93*, **96–7**
 A. vulgaris 96
 A. McKana Hybrids 96
 A. 'Nora Barlow' 96, *97*
 A. 'Powder Blue' 97
Artemisia *124*, **126–7**
 A. ludoviciana 126, *126, 127*
 A. 'Powis castle' 45, 126, *126,
 127*
Aster **118–19**
 A. ericoides 118
 A. frikartii 'Monch' 118
 A. lateriflorus 'Horizontalis' 118
Bamboo 27, *27*, **28–9**, 48, 70, 71
banana, hardy 71, **74–5**
bay, sweet **30–1**, *13*
bearded iris 52, **60–1**
Black-Eyed Susan *78, 78, 79,* 79
box 27, *27*, **32–3**, *13*
branch training 40
Briza maxima 145
butterflies, attracting 142, *143*
Buxus sempervirens **32–3**
Cabbage palm 34
Calamagrostis 130
 C. 'Karl Foerster' 133, *133*
Calendula officinalis 145
Canna 51, **68–9**, 70, 71, 116
 C. 'Durban' 68, *69*
 C. 'Striata' 68, *69*
 C. 'Wyoming' 68, *71*
Carex 130
cat treat 138, *139, 139*
catmint 125, **138–9**
Ceanothus 26, **44–5**
 C. 'Puget Blue' 44, *45*
Centaurea montana 118, *118*
cherry laurel 30
Chionodoxa **148–9**
Chrysanthemum **120–1**
 'Clara Curtis' 120, *121*
 'Mary Stoker' 120, *121*
 Rubellum hybrids 120
Chusan, palm 27, **46–7**, *13*
clary 123, *123*
Clematis 72–3, 73, **76–7**
 C. alpina 77
 C. armandii 71, *77*
 C. florida 77
 C. jackmanii 77
 C. macropetala 77
 C. montana 77, *77*
 C. orientalis 77
 C. tangutica 77
 C. texensis 77
 C. viticella 45, 77
 C. 'ᵛiola' 72–3

climbers, annual **78–9**
compost 14, *14*
cone flower **118–19**
Cordyline 26, **34–5**
 C. australis 34, *71*
cornflower 123, *123*
Cornus **36–7**
 C. alba 37
 C. 'Elegantissima' 36
 C. 'Winter Beauty' 36
Cosmos 70, *92*, **102–3**, 123
 C. atrosanguineus 102
 C. bipinnatus 102
 C. 'Versailles Tetra' 102
 chocolate 102, *103*
Crocosmia 70, **106–9**
 C. 'Dusky Maiden' 106
 C. 'Emberglow' 106
 C. 'Emily McKenzie' 107
 C. 'Lucifer' 71, 106
 C. 'Solfatare' 106, *107*
 C. 'Star of the East' 107
Crocus 147, 152
cut-flower garden **122–3**
cuttings:
 box 33
 pelargonium 140, *140*
 penstemon 111, *111*
 willow and dogwood 37
Daffodils *146–7,* **150–1**
Dahlia 71, *93,* **108–9**
 D. 'David Howard' 109
 D. 'Facination' 109
 D. 'Vulcan' 105
day lily 70, **104–5**
deadheading *83, 85, 103,* 119,
 141, 150
delphinium 73, **86–7**
 Belladonna group 86
Deschampsia 130
Dicksonia antarctica **48–9**
Digitalis **62–3**
 D. 'Excelsior Hybrids' 62
 D. ferruginea 62
 D. grandiflora 62
 D. purpurea 62
 D. x mertonensis 62
diseases:
 blackspot *82, 82*
 fungal 82, *82,* 88, *88,* 107, *107*
 leaf blotch 107, *107*
 mildew, powdery 82, *82,* 94,
  155
 rust 82, *82,* 88, *89*
dogwood 27, **36–7**
drumstick allium *52,* **54–5**
Eremurus 52–3, **58–9**
 E. robustus 59
 E. stenophyllus 59
 E. Ruiters Hybrids 71
Erysimum **156–7**
Eucomis 70
euonymus 153
Euphorbia 26–7, **38–9**, 153
 E. amygdaloides robbiae 38
 E. characias 38
 E. mellifera 38, *71*
 E. myrsinites 38
 E. 'Fireglow' 39
 sap 39
Fargesia murielae 29
fertilizer 15
Festuca 130
Ficus **80–1**
 F. Brown Turkey' 81, *81*
 F. 'Brunswick' 81, *81*
 F. 'White Marsailles' 81
fig *54,* **80–1**
foxglove **62–3**
Galanthus **152–3**
 G. nivalis 152, *152, 153*
 G. 'Flore Pleno' 152, *153*
geranium, hardy 125, **128–9**

G. cinereum 128
G. endressii 128
G. macrorrhizum 128, *129*
G. magnificum 124–5
G. phaeum 'Samobor' 129
G. pratense 'Mrs Kendall
 Clark' 128
G. renardii 128
 G.r. 'Phillippe Vapelle' 128
G. 'Johnson's Blue' 128
G. 'Rozanne' 128
Granny's Bonnet 94
grasses, ornamental 125, **130–1**
Hare's tail *145*
heartsease 154, *155*
hedges: lavander **50–1**
 wildlife 37
Helleborus (hellebore) **94–5**, 152
 H. orientale 94
 H. 'Ashwoods Variety' 95
Hemerocallis **104–5**
 H. 'Golden Chimes' 105
 H. 'Stafford' 104, *105*
 H. 'Starling' 104
Heuchera 125, **132–33**
 H. 'Beauty Colour' 133
 H. 'Chocolate Ruffles' 132
 H. 'Palace Purple' 133
 H. 'Plum Pudding' 132
hollyhock *72, 73,* **88–9**
Hosta **104–5**
 H. sieboldiana elegans 134
 H. 'Aureomarginata' 124–5
 H. 'Halcon' 135
Ipomoea 'Heavenly Blue' *79,* 79
Iris (bearded) **60–1**
 I. germanica 60
Jonquils 150
Kniphofia **110–11**
 K. caulescens 110, *111*
 K. 'Royal Standard' 110
 K. 'Shining Sceptre' 110, *111*
 K. 'Sunningdale Yellow' 110,
  111
 K. 'Toffee Nosed' 110
Lagurus ovatus 145
Lathyrus **84–5**
 L. 'Cupani' 84, *85*
 L. 'Painted Lady' 84, *85*
Laurus nobilis **30–1**
Lavandula **42–3**
 L. angustifolia 42
  L.a. 'Hidcote' 51
  L.a. 'Imperial Gem' 51
  L.a. 'Royal Purple' 43
  L.a. 'Sawyers' 51
 L. stoechas 42, *43*
  L.s. pedunculata 43
 L. 'Little Lottie' 43
 L. 'Munstead' 43
 L. x intermedia 42, 45, 51
lavender *42,* **42–3**
 Dutch 42, 45, 51
 French 42, *43, 43*
 hedge project **50–1**
Lenten rose 95
lighting, artificial 47
Lilium **64–5**
 L. regale 64
 L. 'African Queen' 65
 L. 'Stargazer' 64
lily **64–5**, 70
 African **56–7**
 foxtail *52–3,* **58–9**
 see also day lily
Maple, Japanese **40–1**
marguerite *124,* **136–7**
marigold 123, *123, 145*
markers 55
meadow, annual **144–5**
Mexican Fiesta 79, *79*
Michaelmas daisies **118–9**
Mina lobata 61, *61*

Miscanthus ˈ130
 M. sacchariflorus 131
 M.s. 'Strictus' 131
 M. sinensis 131
 M.s. 'Morning Light' 131
 M.s. 'Silberfeder' 131
 M.s. 'Variegatus' 131
Molinia 130
Morning Glory 73, *73,* 79, *79*
mulching 15
Musa basjoo **74–5**
Narcissus **150–1**
 N. bulbocodium 151
 N. canaliculatus 151
 N. poeticus 150
 N. pseudonarcissus 146–7, 150
 N. 'Carlton' 151
 N. 'Dutch Master' 150
 N. 'February Gold' 150
 N. 'Ice Follies' 151
Nepeta **138–9**
 N. recemosa 'Walker's Low'
  138, *139*
 N. 'Six Hills Giant' 138
 N. x faassenii 138, *139*
nerine 70
New Zealand flax **34–5**
Nicotiana 'Lime Green' *34*
notebook 22
Offsets' 74
Paeonia (peony) *92,* **98–9**
 P. lactiflora 'Bowl of Beauty' 99
 P. officinalis 'Rubra Plens' 99
 P. 'Rosea Plena' 99
palms 48, 70
Papaver **100–1**
 P. commutatum 145
 P. nudicaule 101, *101*
 P. orientale 100, *100*
  P.o. 'Charming' 100
  P.o. 'Elam Pink' 100
 P. somniferum 101, *101*
  P.s. paeoniflorum 101, *101*
Pelargonium 124, **140–1**
 P. 'Attar of Roses' 140
 P. 'Concolor Lace' 140, *141*
 P. 'Frank Headley' 140
 P. 'Tip-Top Duet' 140, *141*
 P.'Mable Grey' 140
Penniseum 130
Penstemon **116–7**
 P. 'Firebird' 116, *117*
 P. 'Garnet' 116
 P. 'Pink Endurance' 116
 P. 'Sour Grapes' 116
pests:
 aphids 76, *76,* 83, *83*
 bay sucker 30, *30*
 blackfly 126, *126*
 cats and dogs 43
 earwigs 104
 eelworms 66
 flea beetle 157
 lily beetle 64, *64*
 rodent deterrents 84
 slugs and snails 76, 87
 vine weevil 23, *23*
Phalaris 130
Phormium 26–7, **34–5**
 P. cookianum 35
 P. tenax 35, 71
 P. 'Maori Sunrise' 35
 P. 'Sundowner' 35
Phyllostachys
 P. nigra 28, *29*
 P. vivax 29
Phyllostachys aurea 29
pineapple flower 70
planting out **16–17**
Pleioblastus 28
 P. auricomus 29
 P. variegatus 29
plug plants 13, *13*

poppies **100–1**
 California *52–3*
 Iceland 101, *101*
 ladybird *145*
 opium 101, *101*
 oriental 100, *100*
primrose, native 153
Primula vulgaris 153
Prunus laurocerasus 30
Purple Bell Vine 79, *79*
Quaking grass *145*
Red hot poker **110–11**
regal lily 64
Rhodochiton atrosanguineum
 78, 78, 79, 79
Rosa (roses) *71–2, 72,* **82–3**
 R. rugosa 83, *83*
 R. 'Blush Noisette' 83
 R. 'Buff Beauty' 83
 R. 'Cornelia' 83, *83*
 R. 'Ferdinand Pichard' 91
 R. 'Hiawatha' 71–2
 R. 'Macmillan Nurse' 83, *83*
 R. 'Madame Alfred Carriere' 83
 R. 'New Dawn' 83, 90
 R. 'Rambling Rector' 83
 R. 'Sophie's Perpetual' 83, *83*
 training **90–1**
Rudbeckia 70, *71,* **112–13**, 123
 R. 'Cherokee Sunset' 112
 R. 'Double Delight' 112
 R. 'Goldsturm' 112, 138
 R. 'Herbstsonne' 112
Salix **36–7**
 S. alba subsp. vitellina
  'Britsensis' 36
 S. daphnoides 'Aglaia' 36
 S. viminalis 36
Salvia **114–15**
 S. nemorosa 114
 S.n. 'Ostfriesland' 115
 S. x superba 114
Sedum **142–3**
 S. 'Autumn Joy' 142, *143*
seed sowing 24
shopping guide **12–13**
snowdrops *146,* **152–3**
soil:
 for *Eremurus* 58
 improving and feeding **14–15**
sprinkler, DIY 19, *19*
staking/protecting plants 36,
 86, **22–3**
Stipa **130–1**
 S. arundinacea 130, 131, *131*
 S. calamagrostis 130, *131*
 S. tenuissima 130, 131, *131,*
  145, *145,* 156, *156*
sweet peas 73, *73,* **84–5**
Thamnocalamus crassinodus
 'Kew Beauty' 29
Thunbergia alata 78, *78, 79,* 79
tools **10–11**
topiary **32–3**
Trachycarpus fortunei **46–7**
tree fern **48–9**
tropical garden **70–1**
Tulipa (tulips) *52,* **66–7**
 Darwin Hybrids 67, *67*
 lily-flowered 67, *67*
 parrot 67, *67*
 T. 'Ballerina' 67
 T. 'Black Parrot' 67, *67*
 T. 'Mariette' 67, *67*
 T. 'Queen of Night' 67, *67*
Viola 146, **154–5**
 V. cornuta 154
 V. tricolor 154, *155*
Wallflowers 98, *99,* 118, **156–7**
watering **18–19**
weeding and tidying **20–1**
willow 27, **36–7**
winter aconites 152, *153*